A BIDOGRAPHY

THE LIFE & (CRAZY) TIMES OF COOL HAND LUKE

Darlene,

I hope you enjoy it!

Jamie Susslin

JAMIE SUSSLIN

Published by
Bella Vino Publishing

For more information, visit
www.BellaVinoPublishing.com

Introduction

My Jack Russell Terrier, Cool Hand Luke, was many things to me: my fur kid, best friend, protector, confidant, court jester, and hunting buddy, just to name a few. He brought me such joy and laughter, and never ceased to amaze me with his intelligence and zest for life. He was so smart that he often taught me before I taught him. At times, he also brought me deep sadness, bewilderment and even fear. I loved that little dog like a son. I considered myself his mom. I humanized him by projecting human thoughts and feelings upon him. I also respected his "dogness." He was my fur child—half dog, half human. I loved him unconditionally and forgave all his indiscretions.

After his passing, I began to compile a list of the most memorable moments I had of Luke's life. I realized I had more stories to tell about him than I had about any person I knew, dead or alive. I felt inspired to share the story of his life. It took me twelve years to get to the point where I was ready to write this book. There are stories with which I struggled whether I should tell. I finally decided that all the stories in this book made Luke who he was and deserved to be told. I decided on calling it a BiDOGraphy (my play on *biography*) as it is the story of his life. It could also be a "MOMoir" (again my play on *memoir*), as it tells the story of my life with Luke. No matter what it's called, I'm so excited to share the many tales in this book. I hope at times it makes your belly shake with laughter and causes you to give your own fur kid an extra pet or special treat.

A BIDOGRAPHY

THE LIFE & (CRAZY) TIMES OF COOL HAND LUKE

A BIDOGRAPHY

HOW DO I BEGIN to tell the life story of the dog who "got it?" The dog who had an innate ability to know exactly how to handle any situation that came his way. The dog who made me cry tears of laughter and of sadness, sometimes simultaneously. The dog affectionately known to me as Studman, Lukemeister, The Peer (pee-er), Lukey Dukey, Lucas Ducas, Lukester and the Studmeister. I'll have to start the tale with my life before Luke. If he could have spoken, Luke certainly would have told me there was no life before him.

Luke wouldn't have been in my life if it weren't for my love of horses. I grew up in the Eastern part of the United States. When I was a very young child, I wanted a pony more than anything else in the world. I think I had every Breyer horse model in existence at the time. I was a tomboy, so I didn't have much interest in baby dolls and Barbie Dolls, but I did have a Dusty Doll and her golden Palomino, Nugget. Dusty wore a cowgirl outfit, and Nugget had a saddle, bridle and a long mane and tail that I could brush. I was an only child with a very active imagination. I spent hours playing with the model horses and pretending I was Dusty riding Nugget out on many adventures. I was an avid reader from a very young age, so I also read as many books and magazines about owning and caring for horses as I could get my hands on. My school's librarian knew exactly in which aisle she could find me.

My parents bought a home on three and a half acres in a very rural area. Our new home, which was actually very old, had a single car detached garage, a chicken house, two-seater outhouse, and to my great delight, a pony shed. On my sixth birthday, my dream came true when my parents bought me a little shaggy brown Shetland pony. Shetlands are known for being very intelligent and also for having their own opinions that often differed from those of their owners. To say they have a mind of their own is an understatement (the same is true of Jack Russell Terriers). My parents had no idea they were preparing me for the day when Luke would come into my life.

I named my new pony Baron. I was entrusted with his care. I was only six years old, but I knew more about ponies than my parents did. During the school year, I would get up very early every morning before school to feed Baron and make sure he had plenty of water. I would then go back to the house, wash up, eat breakfast and walk to the bus stop to head to school. While in class, my mind often wandered to thoughts of riding Baron on exciting adventures. I imagined myself as a jockey, racing him in the Kentucky Derby, or becoming the Lone Ranger's new sidekick. I couldn't believe how lucky I was. I felt like a real-life Dusty Doll. When I would return home from school in the afternoon, I would feed him again, clean out his stall and groom him. Then I would saddle him up or go bareback and ride him until the sun went down. The neighbors allowed me to ride on their property, and there were miles of country roads, so I had plenty of places to explore. On the weekends, I would be gone all day riding Baron. It's hard to imagine now allowing your child to ride a pony alone for miles and miles without your child having a cell phone, wearing a helmet and you not even knowing their route. I only had to be back home in time for dinner or before the sun went down. Baron was my friend, teacher and the highlight of my childhood.

Like a typical Shetland pony, Baron was mischievous. My parents often got a phone call in the middle of the night from the neighbors who were calling to complain that Baron had knocked over their waste cans and awakened them. They would find him rummaging through the garbage looking for any tasty treats. We had no idea how he escaped. He only did it late at night. It's like he was trying to be as sneaky as possible, doing his literally dirty deeds under the cover of darkness.

This day was the day my wish came true.
My best childhood memories came
from my adventures with Baron.

Having a pony means having many friends who want to ride your pony. Most of my friends at that young age didn't have ponies of their own or know how to ride...me included on the day I got him. Baron wasn't one to try to buck someone off, so we would let my friends ride around our fenced field unaccompanied. Baron was a little pony so even if the rider did fall off, it wasn't too far from the ground. There was a mighty walnut tree that had stood for many years in the field. It had a gigantic branch that reached out like a strong arm straight into the field. It was high enough off of the ground that Baron could just pass under it.

The problem for my friends was that Baron knew that. Whenever he had a novice rider on his back who didn't know how to control him, he would head straight for the branch and run under it. The rider would either have to jump off or risk being knocked off of his back. It was definitely trial by fire for those who learned how to ride on Baron.

The winters where we lived could be harsh at times. We would get several feet of snow, and the temperature could fall below freezing, especially if wind chill was a factor. That never stopped me from riding. Baron grew a thick and shaggy coat every winter. He didn't mind the cold and snow either. That was at least until one snowy and blustery day when I took Baron for a ride along a country road. We were a couple of miles from my house when I heard a car approaching from our rear. I tried to rein and nudge Baron off onto the shoulder of the road to get out of the way of the approaching car. His obstinate side came out, and instead of moving off of the road, he backed straight into it. The driver of the car, who had been going too fast for conditions in the first place, slammed on her brakes. It was a futile attempt to stop. The ice and snow on the road were no match for the brakes. Her car's front bumper hit Baron on his rear end. He reared up and threw me off into the ditch on the side of the road. He was scared and ran down the road towards the safety and protection of his shed at home. Luckily, I wasn't hurt, but I was covered in snow and ash that had been used to melt the snow and provide better traction. I got up, quickly brushed myself off and began to run towards home in a desperate and futile attempt to catch Baron. The driver who hit him drove along side of me as I was running. She had her window down and seemed to be quite shaken. She asked me if I was okay. I told her I was fine and needed to catch my pony. She asked me several more times if I was okay. I told her I wasn't hurt, but my pony might be. She drove off, and I never saw her again. I ran the whole way home, terrified of what I might find.

When I got home, I immediately went to the pony shed. I was so relieved when I found Baron there. He was scared and shaking but didn't have any injuries that I could see. I stayed with him and comforted him until he calmed down. As soon as I got in the house, I took my mucky, ash-covered clothes off, turned them inside out and hid them in the bottom of the dirty clothes hamper. I did my homework, had dinner with my parents and then took a shower and got ready for bed as that was my usual nighttime routine. My stepfather called to me from downstairs, telling me he and my mom wanted to talk to me before I went to bed. He told me that my mom saw Baron running up the hill through the neighbor's property towards our house with a saddle on his back without me riding him. They wanted to know what happened. I was hoping they hadn't seen anything, but I also knew I had to be prepared if they asked. I had already concocted my story. I was worried that my parents would never again let me ride Baron alone off our property if they knew that he had been hit by a car while I was riding him. They certainly would have had a good reason. I truly felt like life as I knew it would be over if they were to prevent me from riding. I told them that I had dismounted Baron and was leading him down the road because of the heavy snowfall when a car came along behind us. I told them the driver honked her horn at someone she knew at a nearby house and the sudden sound of the horn spooked Baron. I said that he reared up and pulled his reins out of my hands, and then ran the whole way home. The story worked. They believed me. Whew! Over twenty years later I shared with my mom the story of what really happened that wintry day. She was disappointed that I hadn't been honest with her, but she forgave me and admitted that I would have never been allowed to ride alone again.

When I outgrew Baron, my parents sold him to a local family that had a young daughter who also dreamed of owning a pony. That was a sad day, but I knew Baron would be happiest taking his rider on many more adventures (or under walnut tree branches). I loved that pony. He had been my confidant who listened patiently to my childhood woes and always kept my secrets. He taught me about responsibility, tenacity, independence and friendship. I had three other horses during my childhood after Baron, but he's the one I remember most fondly.

I WAS BORN IN CALIFORNIA and had moved to the Eastern part of the United States when my mother married my step-father. We lived there until they divorced when I was fifteen years old. My mother and I moved back to California shortly after I graduated from high school…nine days later to be exact. We had sold all of the horses by then. Upon arriving in California, I found a job in retail and worked for a year to save money for college. I then attended a university for four years and worked two jobs, juggling work and study time. There wasn't enough time or money to get another horse.

I MET MY FIRST HUSBAND, PATRICK, shortly after I graduated from college. We dated for two years. We were married close to Patrick's hometown. Shortly after our wedding, we bought our first house together. We were both in our mid-twenties. Like many newly married and childless couples, we decided to get a dog. We considered several different breeds, but ultimately determined that a German Shepherd puppy would be the perfect fit for our newly formed family. Patrick and I were both employed as police officers and admired the loyalty, confidence, work ethic, intelligence and friendliness of this iconic breed, often utilized by law enforcement in the apprehension of criminals, search and rescue operations and narcotics detection. Our new puppy wouldn't be a working police dog. We wanted a loving and loyal dog that could serve as a watchdog for our home as well as pull double duty as a fun and playful companion. We wanted to come up with a fitting name for our new puppy, even though we didn't have that puppy yet. We wanted a name that would reflect something about the puppy but also about us. What did we both have in common? It soon came to us - police work. A rookie police officer is someone who has been newly hired and doesn't yet have the training and experience that comes with the job. Patrick and I were both rookies at the beginning of our careers. Our puppy would be a rookie until we gave it the training and experience we knew was necessary to raise a happy and healthy dog. We had found the perfect name. Our new puppy would be named Rookie.

We were quite familiar with the German Shepherd as a breed, but we weren't at all familiar with how to go about choosing a reputable breeder. We were anxious to find the new addition to our family. The internet hadn't yet taken off with the public, so we didn't have it to rely upon for our research. We asked for advice from friends and family, and we read books on the subject. Most advice we heard and read told us to be patient with our search and to carefully choose the breeder. It was definitely good advice. We decided it would be best to meet several breeders and look at their litters to get a better idea of what we wanted. We scoured the local papers in the classified section for "Dogs for Sale," and more specifically for the German Shepherd breed. We quickly came upon a listing for a litter of puppies for sale in our local area. We phoned the breeder and soon had an appointment to see the litter. To say we were excited would have been an understatement.

We arrived at the breeder's home and were told to go around to the backyard where the puppies were located. There were five puppies in the litter. They were eight weeks old and ready to go home to their new owners. The backyard was a dustbowl with no grass or vegetation. The puppies were dirty little dust balls, but we didn't have a problem with that as they all ran to greet us with their tails wagging and ears flapping. The puppies' mother, or dam as they are referred to, was with them in the yard. She was a beautiful dog. We were told by the breeder that the father, or sire, was owned by someone else and we wouldn't be able to see him.

All of the puppies were incredibly cute, but one stood out from all of the others. It was a female with one ear that flopped over to the side of her head. She wasn't the runt of the litter, but she was smaller than three of the other puppies. She wasn't the most rambunctious of the puppies, but she wasn't shy and didn't back down either. She wanted to play with her siblings and also with us. She jumped in my lap and gave me a big, sloppy puppy breath kiss. I wish that puppy breath could be bottled. I would douse myself in it like an expensive perfume. That's when I knew she'd be ours. Patrick was in full agreement. So much for our extensive research and wanting to see different litters. That all went out of the window with just one kiss. Rookie was coming home with us.

Rookie

Rookie fit in right away with us in her new home. She was properly fed and received dog treats as a training incentive. We lived in a two-story house with stairs leading from the kitchen to the upstairs bedrooms. Rookie liked to sit on the stairs and watch everything that was going on in the kitchen. She would sit patiently waiting because one never knew when we might drop a tasty morsel as we were preparing our meals. She was also poised to run up to the bedroom with us when it was time for bed or a quick nap. On one of those days while Rookie was quietly sitting on the stairs, we gave her some ice cream that was formulated for dogs. It was in a paper cup. She loved it and vigorously lapped at it. We soon noticed the ice cream she was eating was coming out of her nose just as quickly as she was eating it. This caused her to sneeze violently several times. I can only imagine how that must have felt. We were very worried and immediately took her to be seen by a veterinarian. The vet examined Rookie and found that she had a cleft palate. It was explained to us that this condition is often inherited and many dogs are euthanized soon after the discovery of the defect. A cleft palate is basically a hole in the roof of the mouth that didn't close properly during the puppy's time in the womb. The hole was between Rookie's mouth and nasal passages which explained why we noticed the ice cream running out of her nose. The vet told us that surgery could be done to repair Rookie's palate, but it is not always successful, and she may have lingering effects such as nasal and upper respiratory problems. We went home to carefully consider our options.

We called the breeder and explained the situation. The breeder told us that she would take Rookie back and refund our purchase price, but she wouldn't agree to pay for the surgery or guarantee us that Rookie wouldn't be euthanized. At no point did we even remotely consider euthanizing her as long as she had a fighting chance at a good life. We knew we could provide that for her. In the very short time that we owned Rookie, we had fallen madly in love with her. We called the vet and made an appointment for surgery to repair Rookie's cleft palate. We knew we would do whatever we could to give her the best life possible while keeping her best interests and quality of life in mind.

Rookie came through the surgery with flying colors. She recovered well and would go on to live a long and rather healthy life with minimal complications. Once Rookie had fully recovered, we enrolled her in a puppy obedience class in which she excelled. She was a great watchdog who kept a keen eye on our home when we were both working the same hours. She was also a wonderful companion to each of us when we were home alone while we worked opposite shifts.

OUR HOME WAS IN A SMALL RURAL COMMUNITY located near picturesque horseback riding trails. Patrick knew about my love of horses and decided that he too would like to ride. We didn't have land for horses so we had to find a boarding facility where we could keep them. We found a wonderful place located only a few miles from our home. We then bought two horses so we could ride the many trails together.

This was Harmony, my beautiful and athletic Arabian mare. We competed in several endurance races together.

The owners of the facility were wonderful people and we quickly became friends. They had three dogs. One was a Giant Schnauzer named Gala. The other two were Jack

Russell Terriers. Reggie was a feisty rough-coated male Jack Russell Terrier who was constantly making us laugh at his raucous antics. Josie was a small smooth-coated Jack Russell Terrier. She was a fierce hunter who was more concerned about keeping the rodent population under control in the barn than she was at visiting with the boarders who kept their horses at the facility. We fell in love with those two Jack Russell Terriers and loved seeing them as much as we did our horses. We had recently begun to worry about Rookie becoming too lonely while we were both gone while working long hours in another town. We decided it would be best for Rookie to have another dog as a companion to keep her company in our absence. If Rookie could have spoken, she would have had a lot to say about that once Luke came into her life and ours. Brenda, the boarding facility owner along with her husband, Steve, told me that she was breeding Josie and we could have the pick of the litter. We were so excited and couldn't wait until the puppies were born.

Very shortly after the puppies' birth, we went to see them. I knew the moment I saw him that the little white puppy with the tan mask with white on the outside of his ears and a tan spot on his left hip was the one. He looked like he would have a broken coat. Jack Russell Terriers have three different coat types: smooth, broken and rough. The smooth coat, which Luke's mom Josie had, is just as it sounds, sleek, without any extra hair on the head, face, body or legs. The smooth coated Jack Russell Terrier sheds the most. The broken coat looks similar to the smooth coat, but the dog has extra hair on the head, face, body or legs. These dogs often look like they have a short beard or mustache. Their coat is a mix of the smooth and rough. The rough coat has much coarser and longer, wiry hair all over. They shed the least out of the three different coat types. We couldn't wait to bring our tiny broken-coated ball of cuteness home. We were very thankful that we lived so close and could visit him often.

The time came to give him a name. One of Patrick's favorite movies was "Cool Hand Luke" starring Paul Newman, so he suggested Cool Hand Luke for the name. Paul Newman played a convict who constantly resisted authority and kept escaping. Those are typical traits of a Jack Russell Terrier. The name stuck, and we called him Luke for short.

When the day came to pick him up, Brenda had a confession to make. She told us that Luke had courageously (and stupidly) grabbed the hair on the fetlock of a Warmblood horse that she owned while it was cross tied in the barn. Warmbloods are a breed of horse that have been crossed with large draft horses and usually Thoroughbreds or Arabians. They are usually very large and tall and would normally be massively imposing to a tiny five-week-old puppy, but not to Luke. He startled the horse who then promptly stomped his foot on the ground trying to dislodge the little attacker. Luke was lifted off of the ground while holding onto the hair but lost his grip and fell to the floor. The horse stomped again and this time it was on Luke as he was coming back for more. Brenda quickly picked up Luke and looked at him closely. She couldn't see any outwardly visible injuries. She rushed him to the vet, worried that he may have had internal bleeding or injuries that she couldn't identify. The vet examined him and gave him a clean bill of health.

While Brenda was sharing the "Stomping Incident" with us, Luke was running around in the aisle of the barn between the stalls. Josie and Reggie were off somewhere hunting for critters. Now that the puppies had teeth and weren't nursing anymore, Josie had the time to pursue her favorite activity of ridding the ranch of any and all critters that sought to intrude upon her domain. These included mice, rats, lizards, and squirrels amongst others. Gala, Brenda's Giant Schnauzer, was in the barn with us keeping an eye on the puppies. If you've ever seen a Giant Schnauzer, you know why giant is in their name. They are the largest of the three Schnauzer breeds and are very imposing dogs. They are also loyal dogs that make it their job to protect their home and family. It was obvious that Josie's puppies were family according to Gala. Luke was an incorrigible little guy who needed to learn his manners. After hearing about the incident with the Warmblood horse, we weren't surprised to see Luke start barking and growling playfully at Gala who appeared very unimpressed with his antics. Luke ran at Gala, grabbed her leg fur and began shaking and tugging on it. He had no concept of the fact that he was only four pounds compared to her formidable ninety pounds. Jack Russell Terriers often have "Little Dog Syndrome" where they try to make up for their smaller stature by acting bigger than they are. I often said of Luke when he was fully grown that he thought he was a 150-pound dog that lived in a fifteen-pound body. Gala, being the stern disciplinarian that she was, looked down upon Luke and gave him a menacing growl, letting him know that his behavior wouldn't be tolerated. She was the perfect babysitter. Luke reluctantly let go and immediately found his next victim...my shoelaces. Patrick and I could see clearly that raising this little rowdy and mischievous puppy was going to be quite a challenge. We had no idea.

IT WAS TIME TO BRING LUKE HOME and introduce him to his new "sister" Rookie and his new house. We knew that he had been socialized and taught some semblance of manners by Gala, but we didn't really know what to expect and only hoped for the best. The car ride home was quite short as we lived only a few miles away from Steve and Brenda and their horse boarding facility. I held Luke in my lap on the way home. He handled the ride exceptionally well. It was as if he had been doing it every day for the entire short eight weeks of his life.

We had decided that we would introduce Luke to Rookie in the front yard of our home. We wanted the introduction to occur on somewhat neutral ground. Patrick went inside to get Rookie, and I stayed outside with Luke. Rookie had been an only dog up until then and hadn't spent much time with other dogs, so we were a little worried that she might not think this new addition to our family was as fun and exciting as we did. She was, though, a very gentle and loving dog. Our fears were allayed when Rookie took a few quick sniffs of her new little guest and then lowered her chest close to the ground, stretching her front legs out while leaning on her elbows and keeping her butt high in the air, thus challenging Luke to a rousing game of chase. They ran around the yard with Rookie chasing Luke and then the tables turning when Luke decided that he should be doing the pursuing. When either of them was "caught," they would tumble and roll together as if they were canine gymnasts or wrestlers. Luke was no stranger to large dogs, so he was more than happy to have a big sister to romp and play with him. The meet and greet was a resounding success.

The next step was to introduce Luke to his new home. We brought Luke into the kitchen, put him down on the floor and allowed him to explore his new digs. He sniffed around for a couple of minutes and promptly found one of Rookie's favorite chew treats. It was a cow hoof she had been working on for a few days. Luke immediately commandeered it as his own and ran to Rookie's bed that was on the floor in the dining area. Rookie didn't find that amusing in the least and approached the bed. She demanded that Luke return the cow hoof to its rightful owner. Luke refused with a growl and sneered at her showing his tiny puppy pearly whites, once again believing himself to be larger than life. Being the kind and gentle dog that Rookie was, she sulked away, but not without giving him a side-eyed glance that said that he wouldn't be getting away with that kind of behavior for much longer. We and Rookie all realized at that moment who would be vying for the title of "Dog Boss" in our family.

Luke was crate-trained as a puppy by Brenda at the boarding facility before he came home to live with us. Crate training makes potty training much easier, and it gives the dog its own safe and private space to relax and get away from things. Luke loved his crate, but he soon found that he loved our bed better. Rookie was also crate trained, but she was allowed to sleep on our bed. Luke figured that what was good for the goose was good for the gander, so he secured his spot on our bed just as soon as he was able to jump up onto it. That didn't take long as Jack Russell Terriers are known for their jumping abilities. Some can jump over a six-foot wooden fence! Chain link fences are also no match for a Jack Russell Terrier. Luke's favorite spot on the bed was at the very top of my head on my pillow. Luckily, I didn't mind it. I think he was able to survey his kingdom from atop that spot.

Mom's pillow is the best!

When Patrick and I would leave the house, we would put Luke in his crate. Rookie was already house-trained and no longer chewed up any of our furniture, so we let her have the run of the house. Luke was house-trained very quickly. He rarely had an accident in the house while we were home. I taught him to scratch at our sliding door to the backyard whenever he needed to go out.

The day came when Patrick and I decided that Luke was ready for a test of his ability to be loose in the house with

Rookie while we went out, without having an accident or destroying something. Our first trip away from the house was a short one. As insurance, we took both dogs out to go potty prior to leaving. We went to the grocery store located not too far from where we lived. We figured, *"How much damage could Luke do in just twenty minutes or so?"* We were about to learn a lot about the little dickens that lived with us.

On the way to the grocery store, Patrick and I discussed all of the things we thought could go wrong with leaving Luke loose in the house with no one but Rookie to keep an eye on him. Luke would often disrespectfully pee in Rookie's food bowl if we didn't pick it up soon after she finished eating, so we made sure that wouldn't be an issue by removing the bowl. Rookie definitely wasn't up to the task of keeping Luke in line. We imagined Luke running amok in our family room, filled with white fluffy stuffing that he had surreptitiously ripped out of our sofa. Another likely scenario would have been chunks missing out of the door where Luke had tried to get out of the house by scratching or biting at it. We had to hope for the best. I think I probably drove a little faster than I should have.

When we returned home, Luke and Rookie greeted us with sheer delight. We glanced around quickly and happily found that the door was in one piece, and so was the furniture. We couldn't find anything amiss and breathed huge sighs of relief. We were so proud of Luke and praised him heavily and gave him special treats for a job well done. I went to put the groceries away. As I sat the bags on the kitchen counter, I noticed there was a puddle of something pooling on the tile of the countertop. A closer examination and a good whiff revealed that it was dog pee. I couldn't believe my eyes! I had three canisters of varying sizes on the counter next to my kitchen sink that held flour, sugar and coffee. Luke had apparently jumped up on one of the barstools that was lined up along the counter. We had no idea he could jump that high yet. He then had to jump onto the counter and either walk through or leap over the sink in order to get to the canisters. He chose the tallest canister on which to pee. Once I gave it some thought, it didn't surprise me in the least. Dogs usually look for the tallest landmark they can find on which to leave their mark. The ubiquitous fire hydrant immediately came to mind. We made a note to ourselves to keep the barstools away from the counters.

Once the groceries were put away and the mess on the counter was cleaned up, we went to the family room to watch TV while sitting on our thankfully still intact couch. I've always had a nose like a dog when it comes to detecting even the slightest of odors. It's a blessing and a curse sometimes. While on the couch, I told Patrick that I smelled the faint odor of dog poop. Patrick and I hadn't seen any little "presents" waiting for us on any of the floors when we returned from the grocery store. I walked around the room, sniffing everywhere in order to find the source of the offending odor. It wasn't easy to see but I found it. Luke had pooped on the highest bottle of wine that his little rear end could reach. The bottle sat on a wine rack on the floor in our family room. I'm sure that Luke was satisfied that his territory was well-marked. Any intruders that would enter would know that a huge dog lived there along with his German Shepherd buddy. Patrick and I realized that our first experiment in leaving Luke loose in the house was a dismal failure. Back to the crate it was.

WE ENROLLED LUKE in a puppy obedience school. We felt it was of utmost importance that Luke learn the fundamental commands of obedience such as *sit, down, here*, and *stay* as soon as possible. Jack Russell Terriers are extremely intelligent and have a tendency to train their owners before they themselves are trained. They will continue to test their owner's limits throughout their long lives. We had previously graduated from a similar school with Rookie, who passed with flying colors. She was a dog who wanted to please us at all costs. Luke, on the other hand, had his own agenda. He had a difficult time paying attention. Most dogs are motivated to learn by receiving treats, praise or play in exchange for responding positively to commands from their owners and/or trainers. Luke…not so much. He did what he wanted to do when he wanted to do it. He was far more interested in interrupting the other student dogs in the class. He was like the kid in school who was always talking in the back of the class, passing notes or smoking in the bathroom. This unruly behavior certainly didn't score any points with the teacher or the other students in the class. Luke was infamous for quickly doing whatever behavior was asked of him during class, and then running over to one of the other dogs with the intention of playing or picking a fight. We never did figure out why he chose certain dogs to play with and others to engage in a fight. I guess it's just like humans. There are some people you like and others you don't. Aggression in Jack Russell Terriers towards other breeds, and also among themselves, is common. It is recommended in numerous publications and websites about this breed to never leave more than two Jack Russell Terriers unattended. It's difficult enough to separate two fighting dogs, let alone three or more. Luke formed his opinions of other dogs quickly. We had to always be on guard when we met another dog. We were asked to leave the class many times and go into a room adjoining the classroom where we would be put on a "time-out." It felt like being sent to the principal's office...not that I would know what that is like (since my mother will probably be reading this book).

Luke did end up graduating from the puppy class at obedience school. One of the commands he learned was "*Heel.*" I used it whenever we would go on walks in our neighborhood or on local trails. After several lessons, Luke would heel on his own without the use of the command. He actually preferred to walk beside me while we were on the road or trails. He wasn't one to stray far from me. He also much preferred the pavement or trail to walking off of the beaten path. He loved exploring, but he wanted it to be with me at his side. Luke was always leashed while we were on our walks. Jack Russell Terriers are notorious for not coming when called, especially if there is a critter to chase. You never know when you're going to run into a squirrel crossing the road or a rabbit hopping peacefully along. I certainly wouldn't have wanted Luke to be hit by a car or getting lost while chasing after prey.

AFTER GRADUATING FROM OBEDIENCE SCHOOL, along with lots of further training and practice, Luke and I attended the

Jack Russell Terrier Club of America's (JRTCA) National Trial which was held in Maryland. Luke was registered with the JRTCA, and this was their annual trial. I belonged to a local chapter affiliate on the West Coast. I made many friends in that club, and we all shared the same love for these little crazy dogs. I think that to own a Jack Russell Terrier, you have to be almost as crazy as they are. The national trial was a way, and still is, for all of the members of the JRTCA to get together to compete and have fun with their terriers. It's definitely not a pretentious, nose-in-the-air type of dog show. Rather, it's a fun, welcoming environment where old and new friends alike meet up for friendly competition, swap stories about their wild and crazy dogs, and let their terriers do what they do best. There are no suits and ties at these shows. Most attendees are wearing jeans, T-shirts or other comfortable clothing. If the weather was warm and people wore shorts, you would often see yellow stains on attendees' socks at just about ankle level.

Mostly male dogs, Luke included, would often pee on their owner's legs or feet. I guess they were marking their territory and making a statement to all of the other dogs about who owned who.

This photo was taken at the JRTCA National Trial.
It looks like Luke was already looking for rats.

There are your typical conformation, obedience and agility classes along with racing, go-to-ground and trailing and locating. Luke was never one to like the conformation classes. He could never understand why he was asked to walk and trot around a ring, stand at attention and not get any rewards for it. The handlers were prohibited from bringing treats or toys into the ring. He was either pulling me towards the exit gate in order to get closer to the rats that were at the go-to-ground site, or he would simply lay down with boredom. There was really no point to it for him. Personally, it wasn't my favorite class either so we usually didn't enter it. Anyways, just like any mom would think of her child, I thought Luke was the handsomest boy at the show.

One of his favorite classes to participate in was Go-to-Ground. For this class, an above ground tunnel is constructed of wood and placed on the ground. It has one or more bends in it and its purpose is to simulate a real hunting experience for the terriers. They were bred to hunt so they have a natural instinct for it. The handler places the terrier on the ground in front of the entrance to the tunnel. The terrier then must enter the tunnel and negotiate the bends until he reaches the end. At the end of the tunnel, he will meet up with his arch enemy. A rat, secured in a protective wire cage, looks eye to eye with the terrier. The end of the tunnel has metal bars to keep the terrier away from the caged rat. The terrier must then mark the quarry by baying, scratching at the bars or silently marking it by giving it the ever so contemptuous stink eye. Luke did all three. It was always wise for us to enter any other classes first. Once he knew where the rats were, he had a hard time thinking of anything else. He was the Go-to-Ground Champion on several occasions.

Here I am releasing Luke to enter the Go-to-Ground tunnels.

Another class that Luke excelled in was Racing. It was by far the loudest, most raucous and fast-paced competition of the show. The course consists of a straight flat track with starting boxes at the beginning and usually hay bales at the end, with a hole in the middle for the terriers to run through into a catch area where volunteers are waiting to catch the dogs as they come through the hole in the hay bales. The dogs are each wearing a different colored collar so they can be identified as to their respective places as they pass through the hay bales to the finish. After the dogs are put into the starting boxes, a race volunteer shakes a lure, usually made of scented fur, in front of the dogs. The lure is attached to a mechanized pulley that pulls it down the racetrack and through the hay bales. The lure is moving at a speed that keeps it just in front of the racing terriers. When the starting boxes open, the terriers race down the track in pursuit of the lure. They are muzzled for their own safety and the safety of the catchers at the finish. It's a sight to see!

Fights often break out between the racing dogs. As they run down the track, they sometimes push each other around while jockeying for position. The fastest dogs who keep their eye on the prize (the lure) are usually the winners. Like the tale of *The Tortoise and The Hare*, sometimes the slowest dog wins the race while the other dogs are all arguing about who shoved who. Luke was lightning fast and won many races over the years, often earning the Racing Champion title.

This is the steeplechase version of Jack Russell Terrier racing.

Luke was good at whatever he did. He wanted to please me, and he truly enjoyed the shows. Over the years, he won many awards and ribbons. I was proudest of him when he won the All-Around Champion for the highest overall total score encompassing several classes. Luke's wins and awards were all in the *12 ½" and Under* division. Jack Russell Terriers, per the breed standard adopted by the Jack Russell Terrier Club of America with which he was registered, are between 10" and 15" in height at the shoulder. There are two height divisions at the JRTCA shows: dogs that are 10" up to 12 ½" at the shoulder and those that are over 12 ½" to 15" at the shoulder. When Luke turned six years old, he was considered a Veteran. The older dogs competed against dogs within their own age bracket. Jack Russell Terriers have a lifespan of fourteen to sixteen years. Many live beyond that. Their activity level remains high throughout their lives. Luke and I took a four-mile powerwalk almost every day until he was fifteen years old. The regular exercise helped to keep him active. It also helped him to continue to excel at the shows and earn the Veteran's Champion and Reserve Veteran's Champion titles, which were similar to the All-Around Champion. It was just for the senior dogs.

Even though Luke was sent to the "Time Out" room during his puppy obedience school days, often for fighting, he performed very well at the shows. He didn't like many dogs, but he never started a fight while at a show. There are hundreds of Jack Russell Terriers at the annual National Show. They're barking, growling, jumping, sniffing…just about every behavior you can imagine for a terrier. If there was ever a time for Luke to feel offended by another dog or have one of them get in his face, the show was just the place due to the sheer number of terriers in close proximity to one another. He turned into a different dog at the shows. He got so excited when we arrived at a show and knew he was going to see his doggie friends. He would walk by my side, pee on my socks and show indifference to even the most aggressive of dogs. He "got it" and knew what we were there for, and he wanted to have fun.

Not only was Luke a Racing, All-Around, Go-to-Ground and Veteran's Champion, he was also the long-standing Dog Food Pie Eating Contest Champion. This was one of the funniest classes to watch. Each of the contestant dogs had a small aluminum pie tin filled and firmly packed with an equal amount of canned dog food placed in front of them. The owners would hold their dogs back until the starting bell would ring and then the dogs would be released to eat their dog food "pie." The dog who finished their pie the fastest won the prize. Luke was so much fun to watch. He literally gulped his pie down in just a couple of bites. No other dog even came close to beating him. It was embarrassing for me in a comical way. The other owners would humorously tease me, accusing me of not feeding him for days before the competition. A first-place ribbon meant nothing to Luke. In his mind, he won solely by getting to scarf down a tasty doggie pie.

The shows were held outdoors, usually at a fairgrounds or park. Because they are outdoors, there are some things that are hard to control. The weather is one of those things. The shows are normally held rain or shine. The dogs don't care about the weather as long as they get to do all of the things they love so much. Another factor that can't be controlled showed up during one of Luke's obedience competitions. We were told by the obedience judge to put our dogs on a down-stay and walk to the opposite side of the ring. We couldn't speak to our dogs or use hand signals once we left them. The dogs were to stay in the down position for three minutes. Once the time was up, we were to return to them and release them to get up upon the judge's command. That day while Luke and the rest of the competitors were in a down-stay, a tree squirrel decided that it would be a good idea to take a leisurely stroll to see what was going on in the obedience ring. Each of the handlers, myself included, audibly gasped. The squirrel had entered unknowingly into enemy territory. Sheer pandemonium broke out when the terriers saw the squirrel. Every one of them except for Luke leapt up from their down-stay and took off in hot pursuit of the no longer oblivious squirrel. The terriers all ended up at the same tree, barking and jumping, trying to get to the squirrel who had almost made the biggest mistake of its life. I don't know why Luke didn't take off after that squirrel. Even if he didn't see it, he still saw the rest of the dogs running wildly out of the ring. I was so incredibly proud of Luke that day. Once again, he just "got it."

JUST AFTER THE JRTCA NATIONAL TRIAL ENDED, I took Luke hunting. I wanted Luke to have the opportunity to do what he was instinctively bred to do. Jack Russell Terriers were originally bred in England by the Reverend John Russell in the 1800's. He wanted a working terrier that could assist the hunters during a fox hunt. The terrier had to be small, flexible and compact, especially in the chest, in order to be able to fit into a foxhole. The hunters would chase the fox while on horseback until the fox would bolt underground into a den in order to escape. The Jack Russell Terriers would then be released to enter the earthen den and "worry" the fox. Worrying consists of the dog baying (barking) at the quarry, which in this case was the fox. The dog should not kill its quarry, only bay at it. In the ideal hunting scenario, the fox would bolt out of the den or be dug to in order for the hunt to continue. If the fox didn't bolt, then the terrier would be called to come out. Some dogs would refuse to leave their quarry and would remain in the hole for several days. That almost never produces a good outcome for the fox or the dog.

The JRTCA issues certificates to Jack Russell Terriers and their owners who work successfully together in a natural hunting environment. In order to earn a certificate, the quarry must be approved by the JRTCA. That quarry consists of groundhogs (also known as woodchucks), red and grey foxes, raccoons, opossums, badgers, and nutria. Luckily this list doesn't include skunks! The JRTCA has an approved list of judges who determine if the terrier has indeed earned the certificate.

I met one of the judges at the National Show. His name was Harry. He invited me to bring Luke out to his local hunting grounds. I was a bit hesitant to take him up on his offer. The go-to-ground classes at the Jack Russell Terrier shows are a great way to let a terrier simulate the real hunting experience, but there are no real hazards to consider compared to actually letting your terrier go in a true hunting environment. It's worrisome to let your dog loose in an unknown area, knowing that he could dart down into an earthen den at any moment to face an uncertain foe, and may not return. It gave me much pause, but I believed that Luke would enjoy it more than anything else he had ever done. Who was I to deny him that immense happiness?

The hunting grounds weren't far from the trial site. A local farmer wanted his fields rid of groundhogs. Groundhogs can be a nuisance to farmers because they voraciously eat the farmers' crops and can cause a considerable amount of damage in a very short period of time. They can pull crops of vegetables straight through the earth into their burrows without even having to come out. They are also a hazard for farm machinery and livestock. Groundhogs burrow underground which leaves mounds of dirt exposed that can damage machinery that must travel over them. The burrowing also

creates holes in the ground that the livestock can step into and injure themselves.

Alert and ready for a fun day in the field.

When we arrived at the hunting grounds, it was early morning. Harry and I greeted each other and I got Luke out of the car. He put a locator collar around Luke's neck. The locator collar has a transmitter that sends a signal to a locator box that is set to receive the signal from the collar. The collar and box are used together to locate the terrier once it goes underground and can no longer be seen. It can make the difference between finding and digging to your dog and never seeing it again. Harry held the locator box as I wasn't experienced with the equipment. I was there to learn, and Luke was there to let his instincts have their heyday.

I was asked to remove Luke's leash. I wasn't used to letting Luke off-leash, but hunting in the field required it, especially if Luke was going to enter the earth in pursuit of quarry. Once off-leash, Luke was overjoyed to be running free in the woods adjoining the farmer's fields. He investigated several holes in the ground but didn't find anyone to be at home. I sure hoped that he wouldn't find a skunk in residence. Raccoons were also likely to be found, but Luke didn't find any of those either. Harry was pleased with Luke's hunting instincts and ability thus far. He decided that we should enter the farmer's fields. He knew where there was a groundhog burrow. Groundhogs are very territorial and usually live alone. They often dig several burrows on their territory. The burrows can be in excess of fifty feet long with many entrances, bends and multiple levels. Groundhogs have very sharp upper incisors that constantly grow, and long, thick claws that they use for digging. They are up to twenty inches in length and can weigh up to fourteen pounds. They are certainly formidable foes for a fifteen-pound Jack Russell Terrier such as Luke.

Luke ran all over the field, looking and sniffing in every nook and cranny. Harry pointed out to me a mound of dirt in the distance. Luke found the burrow with ease. We ran forward to see Luke stick his head inside the burrow to get a good whiff of scent so he could know if there were any critters currently residing there. Luke didn't hesitate to enter the burrow. He was gone in a flash! It was obvious that Mr. Groundhog was home. I felt confident knowing that Harry was very experienced with these situations and had all of the necessary locating, digging and first-aid equipment with him, but I have to say that it felt like my heart stopped when I could no longer see Luke. I questioned my decision to let him do exactly what he was doing now. How could I have been such a bad dog mom?

My fears were quickly allayed when Luke came back out of the burrow. Whew! I was sure glad to see him. My relief quickly ended as Luke turned and re-entered the burrow. Suddenly we could hear him barking frantically at something. Harry told me that Luke had met Mr. Groundhog. Now things had gotten real. Luke once again came out of the burrow. His eyes were wide with excitement, and he was full of energy that radiated from him like the sun's rays from the sky on a hot summer day. Luke entered the burrow again and came out a few more times. Each time he would look at me with an expression of sheer bliss and utter amazement. His eyes urged me to come down into the burrow with him to see the amazing world that was down there. He always walked beside me, and now he wanted me to come with him on this new adventure. He didn't understand that I was far too big to fit into such a small hole. It was hard on me to know that I couldn't go with him to protect him, but at the same time, I knew by the look of sheer joy on his face that I had absolutely made the right decision.

Luke in the groundhog burrow.

Luke looked at me one last time before turning around and heading back down into the burrow to truly engage his enemy. He stayed down this time for a considerable amount of time, barking and growling, letting the groundhog know his days were numbered. Harry said that it was time to locate Luke and the groundhog under the ground below us. He told me that the groundhog was likely only a foot or two in front of Luke. He said that the groundhog would be trying to put dirt between it and Luke, thus digging frantically to escape from the little white dog who had invaded its home. Luke would be digging at a frantic pace himself, trying to get to the groundhog. Jack Russell Terriers are notorious for digging to catch a critter, to escape from a yard or simply to dig for the sake of digging. This was a battle between two natural excavators.

Harry used the locator box to find approximately where Luke was below our feet and also how deep we would need to dig to get to him. The goal was to locate Luke and then approximate where the groundhog would be in relation to him. We would then commence digging with shovels to get to the groundhog in order to dispatch it before Luke could engage in full mortal combat. We didn't know how aggressive Luke would be in his pursuit, but I preferred that he come out of the battle in one piece. Harry located Luke's position and said that he was probably about two and a half feet down. That meant that we had to start digging a couple of feet in front of Luke and dig fast in order to get to the groundhog before it, and Luke, passed the located position. Luckily the ground was pretty soft, and we were able to dig easily. We were just about to the depth that Harry had indicated, and we could easily hear Luke barking. Harry explained that we would now sink a wooden pole into the ground and hopefully it would break through into the groundhog's tunnel. He did just that. He removed the pole, and it left a small circular window into the tunnel. We waited just a few moments, and the groundhog stuck its head out of the hole. Harry had been waiting for this moment and quickly dispatched the groundhog with the shot from a small caliber handgun. He explained that he needed the groundhog to stick its head out of the hole in order for the reverberation from the shot to not injure Luke's ears. The groundhog fell back into the hole.

Luke's barking stopped and we could hear him finally reach the groundhog. I could tell that he was giving it the "what-for." It's like he was saying, *"I told you I was coming for you. You should have given up. What were you thinking you rascally groundhog?"* We let Luke have his moment. To the victor go the spoils it is said. Luke certainly deserved that considering how hard he worked, digging feverishly underground. Harry told me that Luke had certainly earned his certificate. When Harry finally broke through the hole with his shovel and pulled the groundhog from its earthen den, it was a bit heavier than Harry expected. Attached to its tail was an extra fifteen pounds of the happiest Jack Russell Terrier I have ever seen.

LUKE WAS LIKE A CAT WITH NINE LIVES. He had survived being stomped on by a horse, was allowed to live another day by Gala, the Giant Schnauzer, after grabbing her leg fur, and also by Rookie who could have taken him out at any moment for all of his transgressions against her. There were several other occasions that stand out.

We would routinely take Luke to Brenda and Steve's while we were visiting our horses at their boarding facility. Luke would play with his mom, Josie, and help her and Reggie hunt for critters. One day while we were exercising Patrick's horse, Buck, in the arena, Luke decided to come over and check out what was going on. We had Buck turned out and were encouraging him to run and stretch his muscles as he hadn't been ridden for a while. Luke's instinctive prey drive kicked in, and he took off running after Buck, barking noisily and nipping at his hind legs. This wasn't at all what we had in mind. I called to Luke to come to me, but he didn't listen. That's also a typical Jack Russell Terrier trait. In situations like this, they often develop tunnel vision. They forget their name, your name and everything else they've been trained to do. An off-leash Jack Russell Terrier can be an accident waiting to happen. That was just what we were fearing as we watched Luke in hot pursuit of a horse that was one-hundred times his size. Luke was having a blast while Buck was having none of it. Buck got his name from the fact that he was a buckskin-colored horse. It wasn't from the fact that he bucked like the rodeo broncs. He was normally a very gentle horse, but not this time. He had enough of Luke's assault. He began kicking with his back legs, trying to stop Luke. Wild horses do the same thing when they are pursued by predators. We knew that it would only take one kick to land solidly on Luke's little body to end his short life. We had to catch him.

There was no time to formulate a plan. We had a bad situation on our hands that was about to get much worse if we didn't act immediately. We instinctively knew that chasing after Luke wouldn't be a good idea as it would only serve to encourage him in his current dangerous endeavor. Catching Buck also wouldn't work because he was in a serious fight and flight mode. As long as that terrorizing terrier was coming after him, Buck wasn't to be stopped. We got lucky when Buck ran past us very closely. It was probably his cry for help. Luke was right on his heels. Patrick's timing was impeccable. As Luke came whizzing by us, Patrick leapt towards him, ignoring his own safety, and snagged Luke's collar in his hand. The high rate of speed at which Luke was traveling caused Patrick's arm to be lifted high into the air with Luke luckily still attached. We both breathed a huge sigh of relief. Buck got a lot more exercise that day than we ever could have imagined.

We described our home as being "Santa Fe style" in architecture. It had a kiva fireplace inspired by southwestern pueblos, Saltillo terracotta floor tiles complete with paw prints, and a desert scene done in relief on the wall in our foyer. We decorated and landscaped it in a similar style. We planted cactus around the front of the house. It was low maintenance which was good because there was always plenty to take care of with a home on acreage. We always had something that needed our attention.

Patrick and I were working in our front yard on yet another landscaping project when one of the things I feared the most happened. Luke wasn't far from me, which was typical for him. He was probably trying to "help" us by digging a hole or two that we didn't know we needed. I kept hearing what sounded at the time to me like crickets chirping, but it was the middle of the day. I was also thinking it sounded like the *shhhhh-tick-tick-tick* sound of a sprinkler running. Our yard was covered in decorative rock and we didn't have any sprinklers. Neither of those red flag warning signs occurred to me. It was just a background noise until I saw Luke frozen in place, giving the stink eye to something on the ground directly in front of him. I gasped. It was a very large Northern Pacific Rattlesnake. We knew they were commonly seen in our area, but we had hoped they would somehow steer clear of our property. No such luck. It was coiled and set to strike. My mind raced. I asked myself, *"How do I get Luke away from the snake without either one of us getting bitten?"* I thought, if I ran towards Luke, he would think the cavalry was coming in and would have all the back-up he would need to take the snake out of existence. I told Patrick to go and get the other dogs and put them in the house. They would have happily joined in on the snake elimination. Since Jack Russell Terriers are famous for getting tunnel vision when their prey drive kicks in, I feared that the recall I taught Luke at a very young age might prove to be futile in the current situation. I also feared that if Luke did come to me, the snake would strike because of Luke's sudden movement. I felt I had no choice. It was my only hope. Loudly and sternly, without yelling or sounding panicked, which of course I absolutely was, I called, *"Luke, here, NOW."* To my great relief, he slowly backed off from the snake and ran to me. I immediately picked him up. Once in my arms, he began to read the snake the riot act, barking at it with abandon. Luke had obviously sensed the danger posed by the snake and heeded its warning. He "got it" that the snake could do more harm to him than he would do to the snake. I didn't possibly save Luke's life that day. He saved himself.

Patrick and I enjoyed going to a local lake to relax, hang out and sometimes fish. We often took the dogs along with us. They liked to cool off in the water on hot days. Luke loved playing fetch. His favorite toy to retrieve was a tennis ball. He could play for hours if we let him. He didn't know when enough was enough. There was no off switch on him when it came to the game of fetch. I was throwing the ball into the water, and Luke would swim out to it, bring it back to me and drop it at my feet. We played like this for quite some time until I noticed that Luke seemed to be listing to his side while he was swimming back to shore. I wasn't sure if my eyes were deceiving me, so I threw the ball again into the water. Once again Luke retrieved the ball. As he was swimming back toward me, his eyes suddenly glazed over, and he rolled onto his side. His entire body went under the water like an anchor. Luke, like the captain of a sinking ship, went down with the tennis ball still held tightly in his mouth. Patrick rushed into the water and pulled Luke up and out, once again saving him. We learned that dogs can ingest too much water in a short period of time and that can cause an electrolyte imbalance which in turn can cause serious consequences, even death. In Luke's case, he ingested lots of water as he was swimming to return the tennis ball that was much larger than his mouth. Luckily for us, Luke recovered quickly. We learned a valuable lesson that day.

Jack Russell Terriers often know no bounds and don't usually look out for their own best interests. That job was ours and we could have done much better that day.

We had a two-story house that had all the bedrooms located upstairs. We used the guest bedroom at the end of the hallway as a work-out room. We filled it with exercise equipment such as a stair climber and free weights. Rookie and Luke would most often be found there with us while we were working out. They both wanted to be with us wherever we were in the house or yard. The bedroom had a mirrored closet door where we could keep an eye on our form as we lifted weights. There was also a sliding glass door that led out onto a balcony that overlooked the front of our home. On cool days, we could open the glass door and leave the sliding screen open in order to take advantage of the cool breeze that would blow through the room.

On one occasion, I was working out on the stair climber and Patrick was lifting weights. We had the sliding glass door open, with the screen door closed. It was a beautiful day, and the refreshing breeze was welcome. The dogs often laid on the floor adjacent to the sliding door so they could keep an eye on the front of our home. Suddenly, Rookie and Luke began barking furiously. We could see a couple walking their dog on the sidewalk across the street from our home. Rookie, completely out of character for her, began scratching at the screen on the door. She scratched so forcefully that she tore a hole in it. The hole was just large enough for Luke to fit through. He took advantage of Rookie's help and leapt through the screen onto the second-story balcony that overlooked the front of our house. Rookie, like the good girl she was, stayed in the house. The next thing we knew, we watched in horror as Luke pushed his way through the balcony railings and leapt off of the balcony, still barking wildly at the unsuspecting couple walking their dog. We didn't have time to watch what was happening as we had to get downstairs right away in order to collect Luke and assess the damage. We ran downstairs as fast as our legs could carry us, skipping as many stairs as we could along the way. We threw the front door open, expecting to enter a battle zone. Instead, to our relief and utter amazement, Luke was running back towards the front door of our home. He didn't seem any worse for wear. We put Luke in the house and went out to apologize to the couple and find out what happened. They told us that they saw Luke jump off the second-story balcony of the house. The balcony was over our two-car garage. To the left as you looked at our home was the front door and lawn area. The couple further explained that Luke didn't jump straight down onto the driveway. Rather, he leapt towards the front lawn area. The balcony was about twelve feet straight down. Luke extended that jump by several feet by landing on the lawn. The couple said that Luke ran to the sidewalk on our side of the street, barked at them a couple of times, and then simply ran back towards the front porch. That was when we opened the front door. We apologized profusely for the scare they must have had, but they said that no apology was necessary. They were far more amazed at the sheer bravery of the little dog who thought he could fly like Superman. They said it looked like he did it every day of his life. If they only knew.

AFTER FOUR YEARS IN OUR HOME, Patrick and I both accepted employment with other entities. We sold our home and moved north. Our new home was located near the top of a hill with views to several counties. It was situated on three and a half acres. Our previous home was on less than an acre. We were so excited to have the extra space for the dogs to roam.

Since we now had so much more land, we were thinking about adding another dog to the family. Patrick and I had been pheasant hunting a few times with a friend of the family. He had a young female German Shorthaired Pointer that he needed to rehome. Since we didn't have a bird hunting dog, he asked if we would be interested in her. Of course we said yes. We named her Lacey. She was liver and white in color with a mask and a large brown patch on her left side that was shaped like a T-bone steak. I'm sure that would have pleased her to no end. She had boundless energy that needed to be burned off daily. Until Lacey came to live with us, we didn't think a dog could have as much energy and athleticism as Luke. The dogs had the run of the acreage, so it was easy for them to run and play on their own. Rookie and Luke would soon be her new best buddies. True to her breed, she was very friendly and loving, but she also was easily distracted when something caught her attention that she felt needed to be addressed. Like Luke, she didn't always come when called. We were used to that anyway, so she fit right in.

Patrick trained Lacey to point and retrieve, skills she had instinctively. She became an excellent hunting dog, a true partner in the field. Patrick competed with Lacey in several field trials where dogs who were trained as pointers could show their prowess to a judge in the field by pointing out birds and retrieving them for their handler. Lacey excelled at this and won a trophy at her very first competition.

Prior to Lacey joining our family, we decided to take Luke along on a pheasant hunting trip we had planned. We had no idea how Luke would do, but we did know that he loved to fetch tennis balls. We figured that he'd be even more thrilled to retrieve a bird. We were right, but just not in the way we had planned.

Patrick's father, Pete, joined us for the hunting trip. It had been a long time since he had last been bird hunting, and he was even more excited than we were to get out in the field. When we arrived, we initially left Luke in our truck. We figured that we would retrieve our own birds at first. That got to be a tough job. I went and got Luke out of the truck. I leashed him and we set out to see if Pete and Patrick had found any more birds. They hadn't, so we all set out hunting together, Luke in tow. Not long after that, Pete shot a pheasant that fell to the ground on the other side of a very steep ravine that seemed to go on forever. At the bottom of the ravine was a shallow creek with boot-sucking mud on either side. Anyone who attempted to cross this ravine would end up bootless at best. This was the perfect opportunity to let Luke show us just what he could do.

Luke saw where the pheasant landed. He was lunging at the end of his leash and barking at me to let him go. I was nervous about letting him off of his leash because I wouldn't be able to go with him. If he were to retrieve that bird, I had to trust that he would come back. I released him and gave him the command to fetch the bird. He didn't hesitate scrambling down the steep side of the ravine. Once he reached the muddy bank, because of his small stature and weight, he sank down only to his knees. Had any one of us attempted the crossing, we probably would have disappeared down into an almost quicksand-like quagmire of mud. Luke pulled his paws out one-by-one and slogged his way across the water to the opposite side of the ravine. He somehow made his way up the precipitous embankment and found the pheasant lying there. I called to him to bring the bird to us. He picked it up, gave it a shake for good measure, and then ran down the embankment, holding the bird. We were so proud of him and cheered him on. Once he reached the bottom, he crossed the river and muddy muck, dropped the bird and began ripping its feathers out. At this point, we were all calling to him to bring the bird to us. Nope...not in his plans. He gave it several more shakes, dropped it on the ground and then promptly proceeded to pee on it. He let us all know just who was willing to do the dirty work. He sat down next to the pheasant and refused to come to us. I, being the smallest of the three of us, was designated to retrieve the bird…and Luke. I slid down the sheer embankment on my backside.

Luke with "his" pheasant down in the muddy ravine.

Getting back up the embankment with a pheasant and a Jack Russell Terrier who has claimed said pheasant was a difficult task to say the least. Our dreams of Luke as our bird dog were dashed that day.

MY DOGS ARE LIKE MY CHILDREN. My fur-babies. Much to my mother's dismay, I never wanted to have children, even when I was a small child. I know she hoped I would change my mind as I matured. When Patrick and I married, I'm sure that hope was renewed, but I had to delicately tell her that I still didn't want children. She had finally given up asking me when she would get to be a grandmother.

I have always been a practical joker. When we became Lacey's new dog parents, I came up with an epic practical joke to play on my mom. I invited her over and told her I had an announcement to make. I sensed the excitement in her voice as she quickly accepted the invitation. Just prior, Patrick and I were visited by a very good friend, Yvonne, who recently had a baby girl. She brought her baby over in a stroller. We took lots of pictures together with the baby. Knowing we had just brought Lacey home to live with us, Yvonne thought it would be funny if we had a photo of Lacey in the baby stroller. When we put Lacey in the stroller, she laid on her back with her feet in the air, just as a baby would do. Yvonne was right. The photo was hilarious.

When my mom arrived at our house, I could see that she was literally radiating excitement in anticipation of the news she had so anxiously been awaiting. I told her the time had come for the announcement. I handed her an envelope containing a greeting card. She carefully opened the envelope with trembling hands and removed the card. On the face of the card was a baby carriage and text that read, "Congrats to the Grandma-to-Be". My mom completely lost it. She started jumping up and down like a jackhammer, literally shrieking with more delight than I have ever seen from her and crying tears of utter joy. She hadn't yet opened the card. When she came back down to earth, she ran to hug me and most certainly would have bowled me over had I not told her to open the card first. She still held it tightly in her hand. When she opened the card, she found the photo inside of Lacey in the stroller. Her face lost all color, and she lunged at me, screaming, *"A dog! A bleeping dog!"* I practically fell on the floor laughing hysterically. Apparently, she didn't find it as funny as I did. That was the only time in my life the saying, "I brought you into this world and I can take you out," actually struck a chord of fear in me. She has never forgiven me, but at least she's able to laugh about it now.

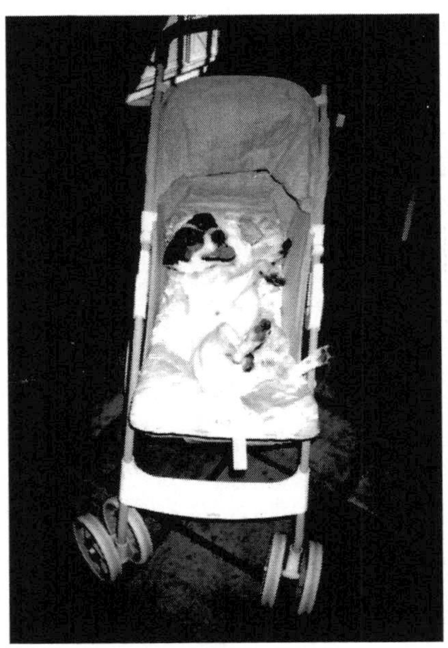

Luke had to have his turn in the stroller.

WE NOW HAD TWO LARGE DOGS AND ONE SMALL ONE. Luke and Rookie had become far less friendly with each other. They fought over things I'm sure only a dog would understand. Rookie probably never forgave Luke for continually peeing in her food bowl or stealing her cow hoof. They never drew blood from each other, but we were worried that a fight could escalate to something more serious. Rookie was so much bigger than Luke, and she could seriously injure him if she so desired. It didn't help that Luke wasn't intimidated by her. Luckily, they never pushed their boundaries too far.

Luke and Lacey got along well. It wasn't because she was his best buddy. In fact, he was quite indifferent to her. He respected her, but he usually ignored her. If she tried to get him to play, he would just wander off to find something more interesting to do. Because Luke didn't seem to enjoy playing with either Rookie or Lacey, we thought it might be best for him if we had another small dog in the family. He was going to be three years old and had plenty of time left to harass and annoy another dog like himself. Why not have another Jack Russell Terrier to keep him company we asked ourselves.

We knew that same sex aggression in Jack Russell Terriers can be quite troublesome, so we decided to search for a female. We hoped the new addition would be friendly with Rookie and Lacey, too, but it was on Luke we were focused for finding a companion. We found a breeder in Southern California who had a puppy available. She was the last one left from her litter. We went to see her, and as it must be apparent by now, we brought her home with us. She had a smooth coat, and her left ear was tan in color while her right ear had small tan spots all over it. We named her Color Me Jade and called her Jade for short. Luke lit up like a Christmas tree when he met her. For the first time in quite a while, Luke played. He showed Jade all around the house and property. He had a new spring in his step. He fought with Rookie, ignored Lacey, but absolutely loved Jade. We were overwhelmed with joy that we had made the right decision to bring her home.

Luke let us all know that Jade was his. Whenever she would squat to pee and Luke was around (which was pretty much a constant as he didn't like to let her out of his sight), he would pee on her rear end. We usually weren't there to stop it, so Jade had to be bathed quite often. She soon got the nickname "Yellow Dog." I often think of the song "*Yellow*" by Coldplay when I reminisce about Jade. I know she wouldn't have appreciated that.

Luke and Jade

Luke was still intact, and Jade wasn't spayed. Her first heat was a challenge to say the least to keep them apart. The dogs lived in the house with us, but we did have outdoor kennels. We kept them separated on opposite ends of the house or by having one of them at a time in the kennel. We decided to breed them on Jade's next heat cycle. Both Luke and Jade were registered with the JRTCA. They have a strict written Breeder's Code of Ethics, along with lots of information that helped us with our decision. We also met many breeders at the shows we attended and asked many questions of them. Luke was five years old and Jade was three. We felt we were ready to raise a litter of puppies.

Jade's pregnancy was a breeze. She remained very active during that time. It was quite the comedy show watching her try to fit her newly expanded belly into any hole in the ground she could find while in search of critters. The day she gave birth to three tiny puppies that could fit in the palms of our hands we made sure that she was alone. None of the dogs were allowed in the room with her. Luke was pacing back and forth like an expectant father. Just after Jade gave birth to the last puppy, I broke out a cigar I had purchased for just that occasion. I didn't smoke and had no intention to start then. I bought it for Luke. I handed him the cigar, and he held it in his mouth while I took a picture. He looked like such a proud father. He would look straight at the camera whenever I would take pictures of him. He was very patient while waiting for me to get the best shot. Once I took the picture, he would break his pose and go on his merry way. He certainly "got it" when it came to posing for photos. When he was able to meet the puppies for the first time, he was very gentle with them. He did, though, miss seeing Jade. She was a very protective mother and didn't allow the other dogs near her puppies for a few weeks.

Proud Daddy!

We had so much fun raising the puppies. All three were boys. The first puppy born was all white. We named him Uno which means "one" in Spanish. The next puppy was white and tri-colored, which was a combination of black and tan. He had a spot over his left eye, a black marking that looked like a Groucho Marx eyebrow over his right eye, and a tri-colored left ear. The third puppy to be born had a large circle encompassing his left eye.

We quickly realized just how much work it is to raise a litter of puppies. We now had five little clowns in dog suits running around, not counting Rookie and Lacey. There were daily weigh-ins to make sure the puppies were thriving, cleaning up after them once Jade stopped doing it for us, supervising play time with our other dogs, feeding, watering, and the list goes on. We had vet checks for the puppies, vaccinations and tail docking. Jack Russell Terriers' tails are typically "docked," whereby a portion of the tail is surgically removed before the puppy is a week old. Not all Jack Russell Terrier tails are docked. We just preferred them that way. The vet must be proficient with the procedure and be sure to leave enough tail so the dog's owner or handler can get a good grip on it when the need arises. Since Jack Russell Terriers were bred to go-to-ground, the tail needs to be long enough that the handler can pull the terrier from the earth by it if the dog is backing out of a hole after hours in the ground and the handler has decided it's now time to go. Many a dinnertime has been missed by Jack Russell Terrier owners who have had to stay the night at an animal den, waiting for their terrier to resurface, especially in situations where the dog cannot be dug out. Docking can also prevent injuries to the tail that can occur during the times the dog is in the ground in a narrow den, sparring with a formidable foe, or running through dense underbrush.

Jade was such a good mom. Her puppies were chunky monkeys.

There were so many tasks, much lost sleep, unplanned costs, and much time involved in raising the puppies. We were lucky they were healthy and thriving. We found wonderful homes for them. The two boys with markings on their faces found homes quickly. We interviewed several buyers and carefully chose the ones we felt would give Luke and Jade's "kids" the best forever homes. Uno, the all-white puppy, was left. He was the sweetest, most affectionate Jack Russell Terrier I have ever met. The puppy buyers were looking for colorful faces, and Uno didn't fit the bill. My aunt Barbara met him and fell in love. She took him home to live with her. She hadn't owned a dog for many years and soon found out that even sweet, lovable little Uno was too much for her to handle. A Jack Russell Terrier will challenge you every day of its long life. Those who are not prepared for this often rehome their dogs or, unfortunately, surrender them to the shelters. We happily took Uno back. We found him a new home with a lovely, widowed lady who had recently lost her terrier. The dog had traveled with her in her RV all over the United States.

Aunt Barbara with sweet Uno.

She even had a booster seat in the passenger seat for her canine travel buddy. We knew Uno would be in good hands while joining her on many more adventures.

Mischievous Uno

Luke and Jade had one more litter together. This time she had five puppies and all were girls. She had a C-section at the vet's office. She was having difficulty giving birth naturally. It was a scary time for us, but all the puppies were healthy. It's quite the job involving a lot of time and expense to raise a litter. It is also risky. We didn't want to lose Jade. We decided that this one would be their last. We once again found loving homes for the puppies. We often received cards and letters from the new owners along with photos of the puppies' adventures and, of course, misadventures. When the last puppy left for her new home, Luke once again enjoyed playing with Jade. She was the only dog with whom he ever truly played, and I believe, loved.

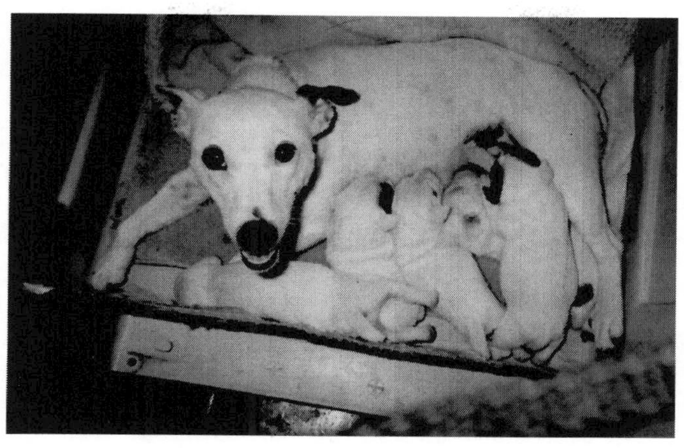

Jade's second litter of five girls.

WHEN JADE WAS FIVE YEARS OLD, she suddenly became very ill. I rushed her to the vet. He examined her and ran many tests. He couldn't figure out what was causing her obvious pain. She was shaking and shivering, and she had trouble standing up by herself. The vet gave her some medication that eased her pain. She was sent home. The next day the symptoms worsened, and I again rushed her to the vet. The vet found that Jade had a rare blood disorder. There was a small chance that she might recover, but we were also told she may not make it through the night. Patrick and I stayed with her at the vet's office. She passed away that evening with us by her side. It was one of the saddest days of either of our lives.

We went home with only Jade's collar. It was heartbreaking seeing Luke looking for her day after day. Since she had been taken to the vet so quickly, Luke never had a chance to see her and to know that she was gone. Rookie and Lacey didn't really seem to notice that Jade was no longer with us. Luke didn't want to eat or spend any time with the other dogs. After Jade was gone for five days, we heard a long, plaintive howl coming from the front of our home. Rookie and Lacey were in the backyard. We didn't see Luke. I looked out of the window in our family room to where I thought I had heard the sound. Our driveway extended out from the house and had a 180-degree view. Luke was sitting at the top of the driveway, looking outwards. For the next half-hour he howled. It was the most sorrowful sound we had ever heard. Luke had never howled before, and he never did again. He was grieving for the loss of the love of his life, Jade.

THIS IS THE MOST PAINFUL CHAPTER I have written. I debated with myself over and over about whether I should include it. I'm still not sure. What I do know is that it happened. It is most certainly a chapter of my and Luke's life together. If he were still alive, I would probably omit it. He wouldn't be capable of letting me know his opinion even if he were still here. I have to go on my own personal feelings and beliefs about our relationship. It's personally embarrassing for me. I think Luke would have had a lot to say on this if he could have spoken. I'll never know, but I think it's my duty to tell our story, no matter how painful that may be sometimes.

I was sitting splay-legged on the floor and Patrick was working at a desk in our office. It was early evening. Luke was sitting between my legs beside my knees, hanging out with me as he always did. I was talking with Patrick about an issue I previously had with an airline employee who wouldn't let me bring Luke on-board with me for a flight to a dog show. I had all of the airline's required documentation and travel gear but was still denied the right to board with Luke. I think the employee simply disliked dogs. I ended up having to put Luke in cargo baggage in order to get to the show. He was extremely tired and more stressed than I had ever seen him when we arrived. On the return flight home with the same airline, I obviously had a different employee checking us in. I had no problems and Luke was able to ride onboard with me. The flight attendant even invited me up to sit in first class, because she thought Luke was the cutest dog she had ever seen. I wrote a letter to the president of the airline about the outbound flight and received a written apology. That employee put a very bad taste in my mouth for air travel with dogs. While discussing this with Patrick, probably for the umpteenth time since it made me so mad, I told him jokingly that the next time I flew I was going to tell them that Luke was my service dog. Patrick laughed and asked me what service Luke could possibly be providing. I told him that I would say that Luke was my hearing dog. I had no real intention of ever doing such a thing, but it made me feel like I could get something over on the airline employee who was on such a power trip. Patrick asked how I could get away with that since I didn't have hearing problems. Since I was being facetious, I hadn't thought about that. I changed my voice to a higher pitch and different tone so as to not sound like myself, and told Patrick, *"I'll say, "He's my hearing dog."* Patrick just looked at me, shook his head and told me that was an absolutely terrible idea. He knew I was trying to be funny, and he also understood my frustration with the airline. I turned to Luke who had been sitting between my legs and repeated the *"he's my hearing dog"* line several more times and asked him if he thought the gate agent would let me board with him, all the while speaking in the altered voice. I didn't expect any response from Luke.

He didn't know what I was saying, and he certainly didn't recognize the strange voice that was coming out of me. He had, though, been listening intently to me.

What occurred next happened so fast. Luke suddenly leapt from a sitting position between my legs and literally flew through the air towards my face. I had no time to react. He landed squarely on my chest with all four feet. All I could see were teeth coming swiftly towards my face as he bit me. I fell backwards onto the floor from the force of his forward motion against my chest. While on my back, I grabbed his jaws and pried them open, as he still had his teeth clamped down on my face. I threw him as far as I could, and he landed towards my feet. Patrick saw what happened and also had no time to react to the initial attack. He sprang from his chair and was able to grab Luke as he was coming back towards me, growling and snapping. I don't know that I alone could have stopped him. Thank goodness Patrick was there and had acted so fast to thwart a second attack.

Patrick took Luke out of the room and put him in his crate. I sat up on the floor in a state of shock after what had just happened. Patrick came back and helped me up. I was covering my mouth and nose with my hand. I didn't know if I had any injuries, but I soon began to feel pain in that area. When the adrenaline from the attack began receding, my body started to shake, and I felt like my hands and legs were made of rubber. Patrick helped me to the bathroom where I looked in the mirror. I still had one hand over the lower part of my face. I was terrified to look. I didn't know if I would be disfigured. I wanted to see but didn't know if I could handle what I saw. It was like when you watch a scary movie and cover your eyes with your hand. You spread your fingers open very slowly and deliberately so that you can barely see the movie screen and the horrors that are appearing on it. I slowly removed my hand. To my surprise, there were only a couple of small drops of blood under my left nostril. It appeared that Luke's upper teeth most likely only scraped my skin. I felt the slightest bit of relief. I walked unsteadily to the bedroom and slid down the foot of the bed until I was sitting on the floor. My rubbery legs gave out on me. I didn't necessarily collapse but I couldn't make it onto the bed. I began to cry uncontrollably. Tears were streaming down my face. I couldn't believe what had just happened. My best buddy, my shadow, my hunting partner, had just attacked me without warning. *"What did I do?"* I asked myself over and over.

I began to sense a coppery taste like blood in my mouth. I opened my mouth, and Patrick could see some blood on my tongue, but he couldn't see where it was coming from. He looked closer and saw that it seemed to be coming from my gumline above my upper teeth. I pulled my upper lip up towards my nose. Patrick sat back and told me that there was a large torn hole where the inside of my upper lip attached to my gum. Luke had definitely bitten me. There was no doubt I needed stitches. We headed to the local emergency room.

I was seen pretty quickly. The doctor asked me what happened, and I told him I was bitten by my dog. I was given a numbing injection and received stitches on the underside of my lip very close to my nose. It felt like the assisting nurse had to pull my upper lip over my head for the doctor to be able to get to the wound. He said it was quite a large hole, and it was good that I came to the emergency room. The doctor also explained that since it was a dog bite, he would have to file a report with the local animal control office. I was at once terrified that animal control would euthanize Luke.

We returned home after several hours at the hospital ER. Luke was still in his crate. He was nervous, and his body shook all over when I spoke to him. He was shaking so much that his crate was rattling like a house next to train tracks. I felt so bad for him. I didn't know what had made him attack me, and I felt responsible for whatever I had done to provoke it. I carried a lot of guilt over it, and I still do. He had never shown aggression towards me or anyone else.

When I had time to reflect on it, I concluded that I either scared him by using a voice he didn't recognize and his fear caused him to lash out and protect himself, or he was trying to protect me from an unknown being that had taken over my body. Maybe he just thought my idea was really stupid. He was the dog who "got it" after all. I wish Luke could have told me what it was. That unknown is something I'll have to live with for the rest of my life.

I was contacted by the local animal control office. The officer made a visit to the home. He explained that Luke would have to be quarantined for a period of time because of the possibility of rabies. Luke was vaccinated against rabies, but protocol had to be followed. Since we had secure kennels, I was permitted to quarantine Luke at home. I basically had to put him in jail for a couple of weeks. I should have been sentenced to stay in there with him.

AFTER ELEVEN YEARS OF MARRIAGE, Patrick and I divorced. It was fairly amicable as divorces go. I temporarily moved in with my mother while I looked for a house. Patrick kept Rookie, Lacey and Luke at our mutual home to not disrupt their lives until that home was to be sold. We came to an agreement on how we would split our community property. Thankfully, there was no debate that I would take Luke. Patrick would keep Rookie and Lacey. Sad as it was, Rookie was probably relieved that she wouldn't have to scuffle with that little miscreant, Luke, anymore. It was a sad day when I went to our house and picked Luke up. He came to stay with me at my mother's home. I only returned to our house one more time. That was on moving day after we sold it. Luke didn't come with me. That must have been an extremely confusing time for him. Luke's life, and mine, changed under our new circumstances. Luke no longer had Rookie and Lacey to keep him company. Even though he didn't seem to care for Rookie and showed indifference to Lacey, I think he still missed them. He had lived with Rookie for the whole ten years of his life so far. Now he only had me for companionship. I couldn't be with him all day. I had to work and would often be gone long hours. I bought and moved into a home close to my mom. She was able to come over and visit with him while I was gone. I also had a local teenaged girl who had experience with dogs come to my home to feed him and keep him company.

My new home had the typical tract home postage stamp-sized backyard. It was a far cry from the acreage Luke used to roam. The neighbors next door to me had two Rottweilers and a German Shepherd mix. There was a six-foot high wooden fence between our two properties. At my previous home, the acreage was surrounded by wire mesh fencing that the dogs could easily see through in order to keep an eye on who or what was coming and going and if it would be a threat. Luke couldn't see through the wooden fence, but he sensed that the dogs on the other side might not have had his best interests in mind. When I first moved in, they would jump on the fence, viciously growling and barking. My greatest fear was that they would break through the fence and maul or kill Luke. Luckily, Luke didn't growl or bark back at them. He knew that wouldn't be wise. Once again, he "got it." I spoke with the neighbors, but it fell on deaf ears. They did, though, agree to split the cost for repairs to the fence to make sure the unruly dogs on the other side couldn't get to Luke. I never let Luke loose outside without being with him just in case the fence didn't hold. I also purchased a large chain link dog kennel so I could leave him outside safely when I couldn't be with him. I hated that he had to be confined to such a small yard and kennel after he was so used to having the freedom to roam almost as he pleased for so long.

This was a worrisome time for me, and for Luke. He would patrol along the fence of our new home whenever he was in the backyard. There were two small poodle mixes that lived at the house behind me. There was another wooden fence separating our homes. The two dogs would often bark at Luke, but the barks were much more like invitations to come and play. As with Lacey, Luke was indifferent to their requests for a playdate. He was never truly comfortable in his new yard. He became nervous and displayed his anxiety by restlessly pacing back and forth along the fence adjoining the side neighbor who had the three large, and most likely, aggressive dogs. He was obviously stressed. I'm sure he was worried for his safety and for mine. Like the typical Jack Russell Terrier that he was, he somehow made those dogs believe he was David to their Goliath. It must have worked because those rowdy dogs remained silent for most of the time we lived in that home. He paced so often and for so long that he wore a path almost a foot deep in the ground along the side fence. When it rained, it filled with water that made it look like a moat surrounding King Luke's castle.

LUKE WAS ALMOST TEN YEARS OLD when I met my future husband, Mike. We met at a fundraiser for hunting and conservation. We had mutual friends but met by chance. We found that we enjoyed so many similar interests, but there was one thing that we didn't have in common. Mike had two cats and I had a dog that didn't like cats. Luke considered them prey. Jack Russell Terriers have a super high instinct to hunt not only rats, mice, or groundhogs, but also other small animals such as cats. There are many Jack Russell Terriers that are surrendered to shelters or rehomed each year because they injured or killed the family cat. Even if a Jack Russell Terrier is raised with a cat, there is no guarantee the cat will be safe.

I found out about Luke's disdain for cats several years prior to meeting Mike while still living on the three and a half acres. I was working in the backyard, pulling weeds and doing some much-needed maintenance. There's always something that needs to be done when you live on acreage. Rookie and Lacey were sunning themselves on the deck by the pool. It was a beautiful day. That was until Luke showed up. I hadn't seen him for a while. I assumed he was patrolling the perimeter or hunting the small lizards that lived in the rock outcroppings and wood pile on the property. I was squatting down, trying to pull out a particularly stubborn weed, when I saw Luke trotting along towards me. He had an extra spring in his step. I noticed he had something in his mouth. It was circular in shape and looked like a small flying disc. I couldn't figure out what it was. I called him to me and gave him the "leave it" command. His jaw dropped open and the mysterious object fell to the ground. I looked closely at it but still couldn't determine exactly what it was. It was covered in dog saliva and now dirt, so I used a nearby twig to turn it over. What I saw immediately made my stomach turn. It felt like I was in a scene from a horror movie. Staring blankly up at me were the glazed-over eyes of a cat. Luke had brought home a cat's face. Yes, that's right. I know it's hard to imagine, but that's what it was. Just the face. I felt so sorry for that cat. We had feral cats in the area, so I'm pretty sure it was one of them. None of the neighbors we knew had cats, and no "Missing Cat" signs appeared on the power poles in the neighborhood. Luke couldn't tell me what happened, but I could certainly imagine. He was a Jack Russell Terrier after all. I had a cat when I was a young child, but not since then. I now knew that I would never have a cat while I owned a Jack Russell Terrier.

Mike never had a dog while he was growing up. He believed that most people owned dogs because dogs were easily controlled (little did he know). He wanted more of a challenge (he should have had a dog like Luke). He thought that cats control you, you don't control them (he was right about that). He liked feisty, boisterous cats that scratched and clawed and didn't take guff from anyone. Growing up, his family always had cats. Mike had two cats when I met him.

I had Luke when I met Mike. I was looking forward to

introducing them to each other. I thought they would get along quite well, even though Mike wasn't (yet) a dog person. Just like Luke, he enjoyed the outdoors, liked to hunt and was always up for an adventure. I told Mike that Luke and I were very much alike. If he liked me, then he would surely like Luke. I explained that just like Luke, I had been hunting since I was young, I love exploring and I have an adventurous spirit with boundless energy. If I were a dog, I have no doubt that I would be a Jack Russell Terrier. Luke and I were made for each other. As it turned out, so were Mike and I.

MIKE AND I WERE MARRIED in a beautiful park nestled amongst vineyards and a peaceful lake. It was a small, intimate, evening wedding. The daytime temperatures reached over one hundred degrees that day. By the time of the wedding ceremony, it had cooled down (if you can call it that) to somewhere in the low nineties. The wedding party consisted of three bridesmaids and three best men. Rather than choosing just one person to be his best man, Mike decided that all three of his good friends would share the duty. They all looked very dapper in their rented tuxedos. They still curse me to this day for putting them in those "monkey suits" as they called them, on a one hundred plus degree day. I can't say I blame them. We didn't have a flower girl, but we did have the very best ring bearer. He was ten years old. We chose Luke.

On the day of the wedding, Mike designated his best friend, George, to take the ring from Luke and hand it to Mike to place on my finger. Luke was to wear the ring in a pouch that would be attached to his collar. My stepsister, Marinna, was a lucky lady. She was escorted down the aisle by Luke. He walked just ahead of Marinna and did something one should never do at a wedding...Luke upstaged me, the bride. All of the guests were laughing and gushing over the little dog dressed in his very own tuxedo and top hat. Luke looked from side to side of each aisle as he passed. Marinna handed off Luke to George and took her place with the other bridesmaids. George was terrified that Luke might bite him in the middle of the ceremony as he nervously fumbled around for the ring on Luke's collar, so instead he placed the ring in his pocket, and when the time came, he pretended to take it out of the pouch. George had nothing to fear because Luke was the dog who "got it." Luke knew that he was part of a special celebration in our lives. He did everything right. During the ceremony, he sat at the feet of the three groomsmen without having been asked. He never once complained about the weather and having to wear a tux. He patiently waited until the ceremony was over, watched Mike kiss me, and then happily joined the party.

The most handsome ring bearer a girl could ever wish for on her wedding day.

SPEAKING OF MIKE KISSING ME, I recall the day Mike met Luke for the first time at my mom's house. He came over to pick me up for a date. My mom hadn't yet met Mike, so they spent some time chatting and getting to know each other. Luke didn't know who this stranger was, but he must have figured he was one of my mom's friends. He really didn't pay much attention until Mike walked out of the door and took me with him. My mom told me later that Luke was beside himself with worry and probably anger too, because I didn't take him with me. He was barking and jumping at the door hoping I would quickly come back in.

We were gone for most of the day. When Mike brought me back to my mom's house after our date, I asked him if he'd like to come in. Luke was ecstatic to see me. He barked excitedly and scratched at my legs, begging me to pet him. He gave me a good sniffing to see what I had been up to with this stranger. I let him know I missed him by scratching his favorite place at the top of his back by his tail. My mom wasn't home and it was getting late. We walked into the backyard to let Luke go potty. Mike had to soon head home for work early the next day. Luke was sniffing around at our feet when Mike leaned over to kiss me good night. As he leaned in, Luke came and sat at my feet and stared intently at Mike. He watched Mike's every move as if to tell him that he had better not even remotely think of doing anything that would hurt me. Rather than closing his eyes when he kissed me, Mike told me that he was looking down at Luke and hoping that he wasn't going to be bitten. He said it was like going to pick up a date and your date's father is home cleaning his gun. That kind of fear. I told Luke that everything was okay. He looked at me and then grabbed his tennis ball and asked Mike to play fetch. Mike knew that he and Luke were going to be buddies from then on.

AS I MENTIONED, MIKE HAD TWO CATS, Lucy and Elvis. They were siblings. Mike worked long hours and was often away from home. His garage was attached to his home, so he left the garage door slightly ajar so the cats could go in and out as they pleased. Soon after we began dating, he told me that Lucy had "left him" for the neighbors. Apparently, they had been feeding her and giving her the attention that she craved. They asked Mike if she could come and live with them, as she was practically living there already. Lucy was a much more social cat than Elvis and wanted constant attention. Mike loved Lucy, but he knew it would be the best thing for her, so he agreed. Besides, Lucy had already made her choice known.

A few months went by. My and Mike's relationship became more serious. I knew I had to broach the subject of Luke and cats with him. I was happy that Lucy had found a great home, but Mike still had Elvis. I explained to him that

Luke was like my son, and I would have him until the day either one of us died. I told him the grisly story of Luke and the cat face. Mike cringed. I explained that I could no longer date him if we were to someday live in the same home and he had a cat. It wasn't an ultimatum. It was just that I would be too worried about Elvis and would never forgive myself if something bad happened to him. I let Mike know I cared a lot about him, but it would be best to call it quits before we went any further. Mike understood my concerns. He told me he loved Elvis but also didn't want to lose our relationship. He said he would figure something out.

Mike called me a few days later and told me that soon after we had our conversation about our relationship and our "kids," he got a call from the neighbors who had Lucy asking if Elvis could live with them. They said they noticed Mike was rarely at home and that Elvis had been visiting Lucy quite often. Elvis wasn't much of an indoor cat. He preferred to keep the rodent population down in the neighborhood. Like the famous singer Elvis, Mike's Elvis was also the king...just of the neighborhood. Everyone knew him. Mike knew that Elvis would be happiest staying in his domain with Lucy. He sadly agreed to the bittersweet request.

WHEN MIKE WOULD COME TO MY HOME to see me, Luke would greet him holding his tennis ball. Mike would play fetch with him for a while and then he would take Luke on a walk around the neighborhood. There was a park nearby that had lots of places for a dog to explore. There were plenty of squirrels to chase. Mike and Luke became a squirrel pursuit team, with Luke leading the chase while Mike ran as fast as he could behind, holding tightly onto Luke's leash. The chase would usually end up at a tall tree, with both Luke's and Mike's heads looking straight up. Mike would tell Luke, *"It's up a tree,"* at which point Luke would head off in search of another critter to harass.

Luke didn't play with dog toys very often. Any toy with stuffing and a squeaker was disemboweled within seconds. Game over. He loved his tennis balls, but he loved one other toy even more. It was a stuffed fleece toy in the shape of a person. It had a squeaker inside of it. We called it "Chewy Man." I kept it on the top shelf of my coat closet. When Mike would come for a visit, Luke would first show him his tennis ball, letting Mike know he expected to play fetch. When he dropped the ball, he ran to the coat closet and then back to Mike several times. He was asking Mike to get

Chewy Man down from the shelf inside. Mike had no idea what Luke wanted the first time it happened, but he soon learned that Luke had certain expectations of anyone who dated his mom. Making sure that Luke's needs were also met was a top priority according to Luke. Mike liked playing with Luke so much that I often wondered if he were only seeing me in order to spend time with my dog.

Chewy Man was the only toy that Luke didn't tear apart. He respected Chewy Man. He would chew on it, squeaking the squeaker so many times I thought I'd go crazy from the sound. It was like music to Luke's ears. He had that toy his entire life. It got dirty and had to be washed many times, but Luke never destroyed it. I gave him a brand new one for his fifteenth birthday. I covered it in wrapping paper as I did with all of his presents throughout the years. I couldn't keep Luke's Christmas presents under the tree before Christmas each year, because he always knew which ones were his and would unwrap them. He never touched the presents for anyone else. He just "got it." Luke unwrapped the new Chewy Man with enthusiasm and then promptly ripped out all of the stuffing, de-squeaked it, and put the icing on the birthday cake by peeing on it. The Chewy Man he had for so many years was irreplaceable, and Luke let me know it.

De-squeaked and de-stuffed.

ANOTHER OF LUKE'S FAVORITE AREAS at the park were the tennis courts. They were surrounded by a very high chain link fence so the tennis balls would stay within the court area. Mike found out the fence definitely wasn't foolproof. There was a dense growth of bushes that surrounded the exterior perimeter of the fence. Any tennis balls that made it into those bushes were probably going to remain there. The first time Mike took Luke to the park, they walked over to the tennis courts. Mike wanted to check them out, and Luke wanted to pee in the bushes and look for critters. As they were walking near the bushes, Luke suddenly, and without warning, leapt into the thick of them. He was tugging on the leash, and Mike could tell that he was navigating his way through the dense underbrush. When Luke reappeared, he proudly held a bright yellow tennis ball in his mouth. Mike gave him the "leave it" command, but Luke stubbornly refused. Mike pulled one of Luke's favorite dog treats from his pocket and offered it to him in exchange for the tennis ball. Nope, no way, never Luke seemed to say as he turned his back on Mike. Luke carried the tennis ball all of the way back home. Mike learned that day there was no higher reward than a tennis ball in Luke's opinion. From that day on, Mike and Luke would return from their walk to the park with at least one tennis ball. Luke with one in his mouth and Mike carrying the rest. If there was no one playing tennis, Mike would often throw the ball for Luke on the court where he could run free. Luke had quite the tennis ball collection to take with him when Mike and I bought a house together.

OUR NEW HOME WAS LARGER than the home I owned near my mom's house. It also had a much more expansive rear yard where Luke would be spending much of his time. The first time I brought him to this new house, Luke was so excited. The fencing at the new home was wrought iron, and Luke could see clearly through the rails. The neighbors on both sides didn't have dogs. Luke was so relieved he didn't have to worry about keeping up his "big dog" image for the neighbor dogs anymore.

Mike and I had to go back and forth several times from our new home together to my own home to pick up moving boxes filled with household items. Luke came along for the ride on one of those occasions. As we got closer to my house, Luke began trembling uncontrollably and excessively panting. When we arrived at the house, Luke was weak and lethargic as well. We left him in the car while we quickly gathered the boxes. I was terribly worried about him and checked on him constantly. When we finished loading the boxes, we headed back to our new house. We decided that we should take Luke to see the vet as soon as we returned. As we pulled away from my old house, Luke laid down on the dog bed we had in the back of our SUV. He was still trembling considerably, and also whining, which was something he never did. As soon as we pulled into the driveway of our new home, Luke's tail began wagging faster than a propeller on a speedboat. He jumped on my lap and gave me wet, sloppy dog kisses. He even kissed Mike who had been driving. His trembling, panting and whining all disappeared at that moment. His state of being did a complete one-eighty. We concluded that Luke experienced the canine equivalent of a panic attack. He must have thought we were going back to live in my old house again. He knew he would have to keep the three neighbor dogs in check. I had no idea how much of a toll that had taken on him. He had taken his old security job seriously. He never let on to the stress he was under. Once again, Luke was the dog who "got it." He didn't want me to worry about him or his abilities to deal with the threatening dogs next door. With the new house, his working conditions vastly improved.

Luke obviously loved his new home. There were plenty of lizards to hunt once again. And squirrels, his arch enemies. There were lots of squirrels. From the squirrel who ran through the obedience ring years ago to the squirrels that always won the game of chase at the park, Luke never gave up in his relentless pursuit of these irksome critters. They seemed to be invincible…until, that is, we moved into the new house.

Mike previously owned a townhome that had little to no outside maintenance required. The rear patio area consisted only of concrete and a few potted plants watered by a drip system. He really had no concept of gardening or even mowing a lawn for that matter. I was much too busy working to have time to maintain the much more spacious yard we now shared. We decided to hire a gardener with the knowledge and expertise to keep our landscaping as lovely (and alive) as the day we purchased the home. We found a terrific gardener. His name was Roger. He came to our home once a week and did general maintenance on our yard along with offering suggestions to improve the look of the landscaping. We adored him. Luke...not so much. Actually, Luke had a severe disdain for Roger. We never knew why, but he did. He just didn't have a way to tell us. In contrast, Luke was friendly to all the other service people we had come to our home. Even though he saw Roger once a week, Luke never got used to him. He would bark aggressively at Roger and jump on him. We eventually had to keep Luke inside for Roger's own safety whenever he would come to work on our yard.

One of Roger's first encounters with Luke was a deadly one. Not for Roger, though. I was in the backyard talking with him about areas in the yard where I wanted to have some flowers planted. Luke was by my side as he often was. Suddenly Luke ran forward and sprang up in the air, landing in the middle of a hedge row just in front of us. He emerged in a flash, violently shaking something he held in his mouth like a ragdoll. Roger and I looked on flabbergasted. Luke had just killed a very unlucky squirrel right in front of us. He promptly dropped it on the ground and proceeded to pee on it. I guess he was telling Roger just whose squirrel it was. Or maybe he was showing Roger what could happen to him.

About a year later, we had some guests at our home on a day when Roger was due to come and do our gardening. It was summertime, and we were in the backyard barbecuing and swimming in our pool. Luke had been playing fetch with one of our guests and only stopped to take a quick dip on the stair into the shallow end of the pool. He didn't like to swim, but he didn't mind getting his feet, legs and stomach wet while standing on the stair. Mike and I had forgotten that Roger would soon be at our home.

We were having a lot of fun splashing around in the pool while listening to beach party music. While standing in the pool, Luke cocked his head hearing something that we didn't, and then ran full tilt toward the front of the house, barking like there was an intruder. It occurred to me at that moment that Roger was due to arrive at any minute. I swam to the edge of the pool and got out on the side closest to where Luke had run. I didn't get there in time. When I got close to the front yard, Luke was heading back towards the rear where we all had been having a fun time in the sun. Roger was standing there yelling, *"That son-of-a-gun just bit me,"* while at the same time holding his hands on his "nether regions." Roger proceeded to pull up his shorts to assess the damage, and to show me the bite mark. I didn't want to look, but I also needed to know just how bad it was. I believed him that Luke had bitten him, but one never knows until one sees it with their own eyes. I recalled that Luke had walked off so nonchalantly afterward. Luckily, the bite didn't pierce his skin. It was at the very top of his leg where his thigh met his groin. Even though Luke had walked off proudly after biting Roger, I think he would have been upset because he missed his mark.

I immediately got an ice pack for Roger. He asked if we happened to have a beer for him. He said it would help to take the pain away. He didn't want anyone to know that he had almost lost his crown jewels to Luke whom he considered a fifteen-pound ankle biter. We gave him the day off with pay and asked him to join the party. Luke spent the rest of the day on house arrest. We got a call from Roger a few days later. He called to let us know he would no longer be working for us. He had decided that some things were far more valuable than money.

Me, the gardener and cats weren't the only things Luke assaulted. He absolutely detested the vacuum cleaner. It was a formidable foe. It usually holed up in the closet. When the monster would emerge from its den, it would announce its presence with a persistent and deafening growl. It would lunge at me and then retreat as I pushed it away, over and over again. If Luke was in the room when I vacuumed, he would come to my rescue, like a knight in shining armor. He would tear into the powerhead, biting it repeatedly and barking incessantly. Several times he destroyed the vacuum hose, by piercing it with his teeth as he shook it violently. His onslaught of blitzkrieg-style attacks would immediately silence the monster and its attempt to harm me. I was never happy when that happened. I'm sure Luke wondered how I could possibly be so ungrateful for his quick action and heroic protection. I had to make sure he was well secured prior to vacuuming. My little hero would move heaven and earth to protect me from the closet monster.

I USUALLY TOOK LUKE to his regular veterinarian's office for his care and annual checkups, but I had heard about a low-cost vet clinic nearby that was offering affordable vaccinations with no appointment or exam necessary, so I decided to take Luke there as he was due for his rabies shot. The clinic was being held outside in a large parking lot. When we arrived, there was a long line of people waiting with their dogs. Luke and I got in line. A friendly lady with a tiny Yorkshire Terrier joined the line just behind me. We struck up a conversation about terriers and their feisty traits.

She was in the middle of telling me a story about how her little Yorkie reigned supreme over their Rottweiler who would kowtow to the Yorkie's every demand, when I suddenly felt a quick tug on Luke's leash. I turned around and saw that Luke had a huge tuft of white fur extending out from both sides of his mouth. It looked like the pillowy soft fur from an angora sweater. He was sticking his tongue in and out, trying to get the fur unstuck. The Yorkie owner and I were laughing at this funny sight. Just then, we saw the source of the white fluff. Just in front of Luke, waiting in line, was a Samoyed. It had a soft and thick undercoat of white fur which had just been diminished by one mouthful. This made us laugh even more. I apologized profusely to the Samoyed's owner, who tried to appear perturbed, but was otherwise betrayed by her own giggles. Apparently, her dog had been wagging its tail in Luke's face when he launched his assault. That fluffy tail must have proven way too much for Luke to resist. Her dog was unharmed except for the blow to his ego. The big dog had let the little guy get the best of him.

Mike took Luke on daily walks. They would usually go about four miles through our community and beyond. They would often encounter other dogs and people along the way. Luke was reactive to other dogs when he saw them coming. He would bark at them, letting them know he had no intention of being their friend. Mike and I worked with him to correct this behavior using treats and positive reinforcement, but Luke wouldn't have any of it. He wasn't overly friendly with strangers, but he also wasn't aggressive towards them. He was choosy about his friends. He either liked someone or he didn't.

While Mike and Luke were on their walk one day, a man they had only seen a couple of times before walked briskly past them. Luke was on a retractable dog leash that allowed him to walk up to sixteen feet away from Mike. When the man passed by, Mike felt a slight tug on the leash. He turned around and saw that Luke was leisurely walking along behind him. The man continued walking hurriedly but muttered something under his breath. Mike thought he heard the man saying, *"I think that little hooligan just bit me,"* but he had a hard time believing that because the man just kept on walking. Several weeks went by before Mike saw the man again. This time he reined Luke in on his leash and asked the man what happened that day. He was told that as the man passed by, Luke lunged out and grabbed his pant leg, tearing a hole in it. He had no idea why it happened but did relate that he had been wearing wide-legged sweatpants that moved around a lot by his ankles. He also owned a terrier. Mike apologized and offered to buy him a new pair of pants, but the man graciously declined, stating his pants were to blame. *"How could any self-respecting terrier live with himself knowing he had let that pant leg attack a man's ankles?"* he asked. Mike couldn't argue with that.

MIKE AND I ENJOYED THE OUTDOORS TOGETHER, especially fly fishing. While attending a fundraiser, we purchased a fly fishing trip that was being auctioned off. The trip consisted of a two-night stay in a private wooded campground with nearby access to an excellent river on which to fly fish. The accommodations consisted of level wooden pads on which we could place our tents. It would be rustic, but Mike and I loved that. Three other couples who were our friends went in on it with us. We were surprised because we had never known them to be outdoorsy types of people, let alone fly fishers.

When we arrived at the site, we all set up camp. We pitched our tents, got the evening firewood ready to go, and then headed out to fish for the rest of the day. Luke came along with us. Mike and I headed upstream while the rest of our friends decided that they would try their luck fishing just below the bridge that was close to our campsite. We fished all day, having caught and released too many trout to count. Upon our return, we found our friends hadn't moved from the fishing hole where we had left them that morning. They were complaining that there weren't any fish in the river. We helpfully mentioned to them that they may need to hike a bit to find a better location. They told us they did just that...except they hiked to the nearest watering, not fishing, hole and had a few adult beverages instead.

It was getting dark by the time we arrived back at the campsite. We cooked over the campfire and enjoyed a delicious dinner. After dinner, I let Luke off of his leash. He ran into the woods surrounding the campsite. Mike asked me what in the world I was doing letting Luke off of his leash. He expected Luke to run away, never to return. I reassured him and told him not to worry. Luke was the dog who "got it." Luke felt it was his job to protect us all. He set up a perimeter that he patrolled like a soldier. He routinely walked around it, keeping all possible intruders at bay. It was as if there were an invisible fence surrounding us that Luke couldn't go over. He did the same thing when Patrick and I lived in the house on three and a half acres. When we first purchased that home, the property wasn't fenced. Luke regularly patrolled the property lines but never left the property itself. Lacey and Jade were known to take unauthorized excursions to parts unknown. Luckily, they always returned.

As I mentioned, our friends weren't particularly the

back-to-nature types. After dinner, we all sat around the campfire swapping stories. The number and size of the fish Mike and I landed that day increased, I'm sure. Luke was off doing his patrol duties. The sun had gone down, and it was getting quite chilly, even by the fire. One of our friends, Julia, went to her tent to get something warm to wear. When she returned, she had a fox fur stole, complete with bushy tail, wrapped around her neck and shoulders. It definitely wasn't your typical camping attire.

Luke soon returned from his sentry detail. *"How did that get past the security line without me seeing it?"* he loudly barked. He launched himself like a rocket onto Julia's lap and grabbed the fox that had been attacking her, pulling it off of her in a single tug. He shook it violently, trying to end its good-for-nothing life. I'm sure he was thinking, *"I won't let this happen on my watch! I'll save you, Julia!"* Mike and I sprang into action, scooping up Luke and saving Julia's fox stole from further damage. Luke was simply doing what he was instinctively bred to do. Luckily, Julia had a good sense of humor. She said that Luke was her very own Superman who had flown in to save the day. None of us slept well that night. What the auction program failed to mention about the trip we purchased was the fact that the campsite was located directly next to the train tracks. The train came through every hour on the hour past midnight, obnoxiously blaring its horn. The sound could have woken the dead. We were so close to the tracks that each of the wooden platforms on which we had pitched our tents vibrated so much that we would have been awakened even if it hadn't been blowing its horn. It wasn't a good night for anyone except Luke, who could rest easy knowing he had saved Julia from a sly intruder.

MIKE TOLD ME THAT he didn't know that he was familiar with the Jack Russell Terrier breed until he met Luke for the first time. Mike said that he had an *a-ha* moment when he realized that Luke was the same breed of dog he had encountered on two separate occasions, both in other countries.

Mike told me about a hunting trip he had taken in South Africa. He was hunting nyala, a species of antelope. He had a professional hunting guide, Andrew, who took him to the hunting grounds. It was a privately owned ranch. Mike met the rancher, David, and his little white terrier who was sitting quietly in the rancher's lap. They talked for a while about the ranch and hunting, and then Mike and his guide headed out in search of nyala. They soon spotted one, and Mike took a shot. Unfortunately, the shot was a little too high and he wounded the animal. The nyala ran off into the bush. Mike and Andrew looked for it for some time but couldn't find it or any of its tracks. Andrew told Mike that they should return to David's home and ask him if they could use his terrier, Janco, to track and find the nyala. Mike told me that he was very skeptical of the little dog's abilities. To Mike, Janco looked like a spoiled rotten lap dog.

David agreed to help locate the nyala. He got in his truck and called to Janco who came running with excitement and a look in his eyes that said he knew exactly what he was being called up to do. Mike was feeling horrible about wounding the nyala and held out no hope for finding it with, in his opinion, this little good-for-nothing dog.

When they all reached the area where Mike shot the nyala, David whistled for Janco to come out of the truck. Janco ran to him and waited for his command. David once again whistled to Janco and pointed in the direction the nyala headed after the shot. Janco took off like a lightning bolt. He soon disappeared into the heavy brush. Mike was anxious to find the nyala and suggested they keep looking. Andrew and David both told Mike not to worry. If the nyala were to be found, Janco would find him. They stood around for about a half an hour swapping hunting stories, but Mike had a really hard time paying attention. All he could think about was finding the nyala. Soon, they heard Janco faintly barking. David told them Janco had found the nyala, but that it hadn't laid down to rest just yet.

Mike was getting more and more worried by the minute. He, Andrew and David all began walking slowly toward the area from where they had heard Janco's barking. Once again, they heard a faint bark, but only once this time. David told Mike that Janco was letting them know the nyala was now lying down.

They walked on and found Janco standing and intently staring towards something in the distance. There, one hundred yards away, was the nyala lying down next to a thorny bush. Andrew told Mike to take his time with the shot. He placed a perfect shot this time, and the nyala was spared from any further suffering. David gathered up his "good-for-nothing lap dog" and went merrily on his way. Mike was in awe and forever indebted to that dog.

MIKE MET ANOTHER JACK RUSSELL TERRIER, although he didn't know the breed at the time, when he was on a guided fly fishing trip in New Zealand. It was raining cats and dogs on the day Mike was to begin his trip. He received a call from his guide, Ed, who asked Mike if he still wanted to go out, considering the downpour they were experiencing. Mike said he did. Ed asked if Mike minded another guide coming along, as that guide's client had cancelled that day because of the inclement weather. Mike said he didn't mind at all.

Ed picked him up and drove to a beautiful river where they would be fishing for the day. The other guide, George, a younger man with a scruffy beard, soon arrived. He had with him an even scruffier little white Jack Russell Terrier named Ruckus. George asked if Mike would mind if the dog came along. Mike said he didn't mind as long as the dog didn't plan on swimming where he would be fishing. The little terrier reminded him of Janco, David's dog, who helped him in South Africa.

They all headed to the bank of the river. The surface of the water was quite turbulent because the rain was falling so heavily. Mike made a cast onto the water to make sure he would be able to see the artificial fly that was attached to the end of his fishing line. It was a bit difficult to see due to the agitation of the water from the rain. He noticed that Ruckus was standing just to his left. His body was frozen into position, and he was holding his right paw up in the air, as if he were a pointing dog. He was staring at Mike's fly as it landed softly on the water. Mike saw a fish rise to the surface and gulp down his fly. At the very same time, Ruckus quickly barked twice. Mike said it sounded like *"yip-yip."* He set the hook in the fish's mouth. He fought the fish to shore and successfully landed a beautiful rainbow trout. Mike noticed that Ruckus had moved on to other more interesting things. After admiring the magnificent trout, Mike released it back into the water. He moved several yards downriver to cast for another fish. He noticed that Ruckus had rejoined him, once again standing by his side and pointing. Mike asked George just what in the world it was that Ruckus was doing. George laughed and told Mike that Ruckus was his "strike indicator" for clients who couldn't see well or didn't know when a fish had risen and eaten the fly they had casted. A strike indicator is similar to a bobber, but is used by fly fishers. It lets the fly fisher know when a fish has eaten a fly. Ruckus would watch the fly as it hit the water. When a fish ate the fly, Ruckus would bark twice. This would let the fishing client know to set the hook in the fish's mouth. Mike was an experienced fly fisherman, but he was certainly happy to have Ruckus along that day. With the rain as heavy as it was, it certainly helped to have another set of eyes on the fly. Mike had one of his most successful days of fly fishing. He gave much of the credit for his accomplishments in landing some of the most impressive rainbow trout that day to Ruckus, the canine strike indicator.

MIKE AND I LOVED TO HIKE. We would often spend our weekends exploring scenic trails. We were lucky to live in close proximity to the mountains and beaches. If we left early in the morning, we could be on the trail with plenty of time to enjoy all that nature had to offer. Luke was the perfect hiking partner. He had way more energy than we did. We didn't have to worry about tiring him out. As far as we were concerned, a tired Jack Russell Terrier was a good Jack Russell Terrier. Luke enjoyed sniffing around along the trails. There were many new scents to discover. Depending upon where we were hiking, whether it be in the mountains or along the beach, there were also many new critters to see. We encountered coyotes, skunks, squirrels, starfish and deer, just to name a few.

Prior to meeting Mike, while on a hike, alone in the woods with Luke when he was only two years old, I saw a coyote not too far ahead of us on the trail. It didn't look healthy. Its coat was scraggly, and it appeared emaciated. It didn't run off as we approached. I yelled at it, stomped my feet and waved my arms in the air to scare it away, but it didn't budge. I was worried that it might be rabid and try to attack us. I didn't want Luke to see it, though I knew he would because of my strange behavior. I thought he might start barking and growling at the coyote and cause it to come after us. After all, it wasn't frightened by my threatening gestures. When Luke did see the coyote, not a peep came out of him. He moved from my side to the end of his leash, closer to the coyote, and stood squarely facing it. He was letting the coyote know that it would have to come through him first if it wanted to get to me. I believe that he didn't bark because he didn't want to show any fear. He only wanted to protect me, and his fear would only make us appear more vulnerable. I was afraid, and Luke sensed it. I started to walk backwards, always keeping an eye on the coyote who was following us. Luke stayed at the end of his leash, closer to the coyote, never taking his eyes off of it. We walked that way for almost a mile, with the coyote matching our every step. It was unnerving to say the least. When we got close to the road where the trail began, the coyote suddenly ran away into the woods. I think Luke and I both breathed a huge sigh of relief. This was another of those times that Luke "got it." He knew the coyote could attack either of us at any moment, and he chose to stand his ground and protect his mom, all by not overreacting to the threat. His silent but deadly approach may have instilled enough fear into the coyote to keep it at bay. It was certainly much bigger than Luke. He never knew his size.

WHEN LUKE WAS ELEVEN YEARS OLD, Mike and I took him on a hike. It was a beautiful day and the temperature was in the low seventies...a perfect day to hike. The trail meandered through a wooded area with lots of things for Luke to see and sniff, along with plenty of low bushes and trees that needed to be peed upon. Luke was an excellent outdoor guide and always left behind a yellow breadcrumb trail that we could follow back to the car in case we got lost.

The trail reached a very steep upward slope with a rapid gain in elevation. It consisted mostly of low-lying shrubs, scree and boulders. We hoped the view from the top would be well worth the effort we knew it would take to reach the summit. We decided to begin our ascent. Luke was in the lead on-leash, with Mike closely following. I was taking my time, being mindful to choose the best route to the top. I was, and still am, deathly afraid of heights. I can't remember a time when I wasn't afraid of heights. It's an irrational fear. I've spoken with many other people who have this same fear and found that we all experience it quite differently. When I stand too close to the edge of a canyon for instance, my legs feel like rubber, my body trembles uncontrollably, and I experience shortness of breath and a sense of vertigo. All I want to do is get as far away from the edge (the death zone in my opinion) as I can possibly get. On the other hand, I have been skydiving twice and have bungee jumped several times. I really can't explain why those activities don't instill the same dread in me. As I said, it's completely irrational. No one can talk me out of it either. It irritates me to no end when someone tells me there's nothing to be afraid of or that I'm completely safe. More on that later.

The three of us reached an area where we had to scramble up and over boulders in order to reach the top. I was doing fine until we came upon a rock face that we couldn't climb. The only way we could get to the summit was to inch our way around the rock face along a narrow ledge, while trying to find a good place to grip with our fingers on the sheer rock wall. That's when the terror crept deep into my bones. I immediately looked down (big mistake) and saw that there was no way I was going to be able to go back down the way we had come. It was way too steep. At least it was in my opinion. I looked again at the rock face. It stared back at me with a toothy, menacing grin, threatening to push me over the edge if I attempted to go around. I couldn't go up, and I couldn't go down. There was nowhere I could sit in order to try to calm down. I began to have a panic attack, and my reaction was to freeze in place. Mike kept telling me that I was totally safe and he would help me once he was able to get around the rock face. That only served to seriously annoy me. I told him that he had better go on without me and call in a helicopter for a rescue mission.

When we reached the rock face, Luke was panting heavily and was slowing down considerably. He needed a break, too. This was one of the few times we saw Luke visibly tired. Mike knew that he and Luke had to keep going and that I would hopefully follow once I was able to calm down enough to consider my options. He realized after I had thrown some not-so-nice expletives his way that assuring me I was safe wasn't, literally and figuratively, gaining any ground.

Luke had never liked to be carried. He wanted to be large and in-charge. That is one of the reasons I didn't pick him up and carry him when we encountered the coyote so many years ago. This time was different. Luke needed a helping hand in order to get to the top. He happily let Mike pick him up. He climbed up onto Mike's shoulder, looked at me, looked onwards and upwards, and then they both disappeared around the rock face. I couldn't watch. I was terrified. I just knew they were both going to tumble down the rocky, steep slope to their grisly, inevitable deaths below. Of course, that didn't happen. After some time, I was able to regain my senses and realize that a helicopter was out of the question. If Mike was able to make it around the rock face while carrying Luke, well then, I would have to take my chances. I don't remember actually doing it. I think my brain protected me from myself. Somehow, I managed to inch my way around the rock face. Mike and Luke were there waiting for me. We had to scramble to the top up and over many more boulders. Mike was still carrying Luke who was looking at me and then to the summit and back again. It was as if he was telling me that I could make it and the effort would be entirely worth it.

Once we reached the summit, we were treated to a spectacular 360-degree view of mountains, golden meadows and valleys as far as the eye could see. Mike let Luke off of his leash. He figured he was too tired to run away. Luke immediately ran to the highest boulder he could climb in order to get a better view. After all, he was only twelve and a half inches high. Mike and I both watched as Luke gazed out over what I'm sure he thought was his kingdom. We were all in awe of the magnificent scene before us. Luke sat perched upon the boulder for twenty minutes, looking in all directions. He knew we all had worked hard to get there. At that moment, I think he was appreciating all of the effort and the glorious reward at the end. Once again, he "got it."

Luke surveying his kingdom.

LUKE HAD PROVEN that Mike's pre-conceived notions about dogs were wrong. Luke definitely wasn't easy to control, and he was constantly challenging us in every way he possibly could. He always kept us guessing his next move. He also made us laugh at his many antics. He was like a clown wearing a dog suit. Mike loved all of these attributes about Luke. He had to admit that Luke had turned him into a dog person. He still loved cats, but he knew that we couldn't safely bring a cat into our family as long as Luke was around. He also knew that Luke was my dog. Mike had missed out on Luke's younger years. He wanted to raise a dog from puppyhood just as I had.

WE DECIDED THAT WE SHOULD LOOK FOR A FEMALE Jack Russell Terrier to add to our family, keep Luke company, and be Mike's "daddy's girl." Luke had gone from, at one time, a pack of four dogs, to being an only dog. Even though he didn't like Rookie and only tolerated Lacey, he did love Jade. Luke was twelve years old and still full of more energy than a dog should have. Many Jack Russell Terrier owners report that their dogs never slowed down throughout their lifetimes. The time was right to find the next addition to our family.

Rather than purchasing a puppy from a breeder this time, we decided to search for a rescue dog in need of a home. I searched online every day for female Jack Russell Terriers under one-year of age. There weren't many available, and when there were, they were often adopted before we even had a chance to see them. It got to the point where I was hesitant to tell Mike about a dog until I found out if it was still available. We did see a couple of dogs, but they didn't fit in for one reason or another with our family.

Almost two months into my search, I saw a photo online of an adorable little white puppy with a bit of black coloring on her ears and an almost perfectly round black spot on her back. Mike had come into the room behind me while I was searching and looked over my shoulder at the computer screen. He gave me a start when he loudly exclaimed, *"That's the one! You need to call about her right away."* He knew he wanted her from the very first time her saw her. It was love at first sight.

I immediately made the call and reached Trish, the woman who was kindly fostering her. She told me the dog's name was Cricket and she had been found wandering outside in the parking lot of the local police department in the city where Trish lived. Many of the police officers at the department knew Trish and that she had rescued many animals over the years, so they called and asked her to help care for and find a home for the wandering little puppy. No one had come to claim her, so Trish put her on a national website where prospective adopters could go to search for animals in need of a forever home. Trish took Cricket to the vet and got an exam and vaccinations. She was told that Cricket was most likely six months old. I asked if we could come to see her. Trish delivered the bad news we had heard time and time again. She explained that a couple with small children would be arriving within a couple of hours, and she fully expected they would take Cricket home with them. I told her how much that saddened me to hear as we had been looking for quite some time for just such a dog. I told her how much Luke had loved Jade and how despondent he was after losing her. I had read in Cricket's online "bio" before placing the call to Trish about how Trish thought she would make an excellent agility dog. I related to Trish that Luke had competed in agility and there was even a photo of Luke and me competing at a show in a book about Jack Russell Terriers. I let her know that I was very familiar with the breed and knew how to protect these little dogs from themselves, as they can be their own worst enemies. I told her that it sounded like Cricket would be the perfect dog for us and to please let me know if she was still available after the family came to see her. Trish promised she would.

I delivered the bad news once again to Mike. He dejectedly lowered his head and went out to mow the lawn. He had gotten his hopes up about this one. About fifteen minutes later, our phone rang. It was Trish. She sounded very worried. She told me that after we had spoken, she talked with her husband and told him that she felt we would be a much better match for Cricket than the family who would soon be on their way to see her. He asked her why she was even hesitating in calling us back if she truly felt that way. She asked if it would be possible for us to come right away. I explained that we lived three hours away, but we would leave immediately if she would wait for us. Trish said that she had never cancelled an appointment before with a prospective adopter, but she would do it this time because she felt that Cricket would have a wonderful breed-appropriate home with us. She said she felt awful calling the other family and cancelling on them. She told me she was going to say that Cricket had suddenly become ill. She said that just saying all of that was making her feel ill. I told her we wouldn't let her, or Cricket, down.

After hanging up the phone, I ran to the backyard and gave Mike the good news. He practically jumped for joy. He turned off the lawn mower, ran inside to put on clean clothes, grabbed the checkbook and Luke, and off we headed to meet Cricket.

When we arrived at Trish's home, we saw that she had Cricket off-leash outside in a large, fenced field. We introduced ourselves and thanked her profusely for giving us the opportunity to meet Cricket. Cricket was running around the field looking for critters. She was a girl after Luke's own heart. We brought him out and introduced them. Luke was strutting around, showing Cricket just how cool and handsome of a ladies' man he was. He looked from her to me as if to ask if she could please come home with us. Cricket proceeded to show him all of the critter holes in the field.

I told Trish that I wanted to do some temperament testing on Cricket to make sure she would fit in with our family dynamics. Trish suggested that we take Cricket to a horse stall in the barn where Cricket had been staying while living with her. I wanted to see how Cricket reacted to a variety of situations and sounds. One of the tests involved me opening an automatic umbrella close to Cricket and placing it on the ground. Cricket didn't even flinch as the umbrella flew open. She ran over to it, gave it a quick sniff, and then proceeded to get one of the many toys she had in the stall. She passed the tests with flying colors. She wasn't afraid of anything. Trish explained that Cricket loved to play with toys. She had taken toys from several other dogs that Trish had rescued and put them in her stall. She had quite the collection. When Luke came into the stall after I finished the temperament testing, Cricket gathered all of her toys and placed them on her dog bed. Sharing obviously wasn't her strongest suit. Even so, she and Luke got along very well. He was more interested in playing with her than with her toys anyways. We told Trish we would love to give Cricket her forever home.

Trish had an adoption form that she needed us to fill out. It stated amongst other things that we would have Cricket spayed at our first opportunity. She required a hefty spay deposit that would be returned to us upon our providing proof of the spay. We readily agreed to all of her terms as they were meant to be in Cricket's best interest. Trish and I went inside her home so I could complete the paperwork and pay for Cricket. Mike took Luke and her to our car. I copiously thanked Trish for giving us the opportunity to provide Cricket with her forever home. Trish said she would always feel guilty about the little white lie she had told to the other family, but she knew that Cricket would be happiest with us, and she felt she was doing the right thing. Little did she know she had made the right decision. We soon found that Cricket wasn't friendly with children and couldn't be trusted with them. It's possible she had a bad experience with a child prior to being rescued. Since dogs can't talk, we'll never know. That family may have been saved from an unfortunate and dangerous situation. Hopefully they found a family-friendly dog who didn't mind a little ear-tugging every now and then.

When I got in the car to go home, Cricket was sleeping in Mike's lap. He told me that when he got in the car with both dogs, Luke sat on the passenger seat and Cricket climbed onto his lap. She laid down and let out a long sigh of relief. It seemed she knew she had found a safe and happy home. On the way to our house, we stopped at a big box pet store and bought an armful of dog toys. There wasn't a toy in our home except for Chewy Man, of course, that Luke hadn't unstuffed and de-squeaked. We knew from our visit to her stall that wouldn't have been acceptable to Cricket.

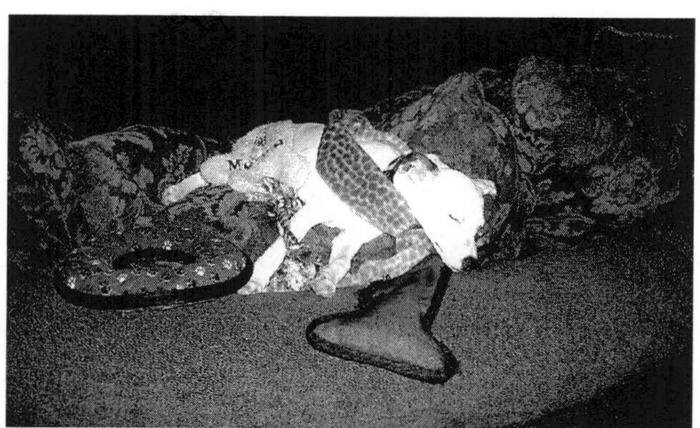

An exhausted Bella (Cricket) after collecting several of her many toys.

We liked her name, but we wanted to give her a name of our own. We thought of many names, but Bella was the one that stood out. It means "pretty" in Italian. We thought we had come up with an original name. It turns out we were wrong…really wrong. The first time we took Bella and Luke to a dog park, we heard at least three different owners calling their Bella to come to them. I went home and searched online for popular dog names and found that Bella was the most popular female dog name that year. Oh well, we still loved the name and thought she was the prettiest little girl. As Bella got a bit older, we realized she was most likely a Rat Terrier. They share many of the same traits with Jack Russell Terriers, but Rat Terriers are often bigger and have ears that are erect rather than folding over. They also don't bark as much. Bella's ears flopped over when we got her, but soon began to stand up on their own. Her size and body type also indicated Rat Terrier. One difference we noticed between Bella and Luke was that Bella thought before she acted, and Luke acted before he thought. I think that's probably a common difference between Rat Terriers and Jack Russell Terriers. Since Bella was a rescue dog, we would never know for sure. One thing we did know was that neither we, nor Luke, cared about that. We all loved her and were happy she was a member of our family.

BELLA'S SECOND FAVORITE THING IN LIFE besides her toys was swimming in our pool. Luke came in a distant third. She swam so much we called her the Mark Spitz of the dog world. She could swim for an hour without getting out of the pool or stopping to rest. One of the first things we had to teach her was how

Bella had typical, erect Rat Terrier ears.

to get out of the pool. Once she learned that, we could safely let her out into our backyard without having to be out there with her. Luke also knew how to get out of the pool, but swimming wasn't his thing. He preferred to bark at her from the edge of the pool while she swam. I liked to imagine he was cheering her on during the Olympics while she was vying for the gold medal.

There was a small lake within our community. We passed by it often on our daily walks with Luke and Bella. On hot and sunny days, Bella would pull us over to the lake and jump in. She couldn't swim very far on her leash, so one day we thought it would be a good idea to let her swim without it. Mike released the leash from her collar, and she leapt into the water like a competition swimmer launching from a starting block. She was having a blast swimming around the lake. We had an important appointment to make soon, so we called to Bella to come in from swimming. She glanced at us and then completely ignored any further commands to come to shore. We called and called to her, but it seemed she had forgotten her name. Since she could swim for at least an hour, we knew we were in trouble. I suddenly remembered a time Mike had been fishing in the lake. As he was bringing the fish to shore, Bella saw it moving around in the water, so I took her over to investigate. Her prey instincts kicked in, and she jumped in the water to try to catch the fish. Luckily, she was on a leash and I was able to quickly pull her back in to the shore. I told Mike to run home and get his fishing rod. I had an idea that just might work. Mike came back with a bobber attached to the end of his line. He made a couple of casts to get Bella's attention. It worked. She swam right to him as he reeled in the "fish." We made it to our appointment on time and learned never to let our crazy little water dog go for a swim when we had somewhere to go.

Apparently, we didn't learn our lesson with Bella well enough. We visited a dog park on a particularly hot and sweltering day. Luke had been playing fetch with Mike while Bella wandered around exploring the park. She didn't enjoy playing with any dogs other than Luke. She never fought with another dog either. It seemed other dogs just knew she wasn't interested in playing, so they kept their distance. That was just fine with Bella. She preferred it that way. When we left the dog park, both dogs were panting heavily, even though they drank copious amounts of water. We hosed them off to cool them down using the hose provided at the park. Just outside of the gate to the park was a lake. Knowing how much Bella liked to swim and considering how hot it was outside, I got the not-so-bright idea to let her off of her leash so she could cool off in the water. I should have learned my lesson the first time.

As Bella ran excitedly towards the pond, I noticed there

was a mother duck with eight ducklings paddling around on the opposite side of the lake. The unfortunate thing was that Bella saw them too. I called to her to come back to me, knowing full well my calls were falling on deaf ears. Bella leapt into the water and began swimming directly towards the ducks. The mother duck protectively called all of her ducklings to her. There was a family with three small children picnicking near the shore, watching the horror show that was unfolding before their eyes. The kids were screaming and crying, worried about the fate of the ducks. As Bella got nearer to the ducks, the ducklings panicked and separated from their mother. Pandemonium ensued as the mother duck tried unsuccessfully to distract Bella from her babies.

It all happened so fast. I had little time to react. Mike held onto Luke who was barking furiously, most certainly rooting for Bella, while I quickly removed my shoes and emptied my pockets. I stepped into the pond fully clothed. I never swam before without properly wearing a swimsuit, and I have no intention of ever doing it again. It wasn't easy. I deserved it though, due to my poor judgment by letting Bella off-leash to take a cooling dip in the lake. My feet sank deep down into the mud at the bottom of the pond near the shore. They felt like they had been sucked into the mouth of an eel. I began to swim towards Bella who had no intention of coming to me. She was trying her best to catch the ducklings. Luckily, they were surprisingly fast. They seemed to have an extra gear that came in handy in situations such as they currently found themselves. I, too, was lucky. I had been on the swim team in high school. The training I gained there paid off when I was able to outswim my duck-crazed little terrier. I was able to grab Bella's collar and tug her back to shore. It was no easy task. She only weighed twenty pounds, but that was plenty to deal with considering she fought me every inch of the way back. Mike and I, along with the family who watched the frantic scene, all breathed a huge sigh of relief. The ride home was a cold one. There were no towels in our car with which to dry myself off. Mike had the air conditioning set to high as it was over ninety degrees outside, and he and Luke were very hot. I swore to myself at that moment I would never again give Bella the opportunity to pretend she couldn't hear me. Anyone within a mile's radius of that park probably heard us calling to her that day. A terrier's prey drive is so instinctually ingrained. One never knows when a critter will present itself. Letting Bella or Luke off-leash always required a serious leap of faith, and the willingness to extricate them from any situation they may have gotten themselves into. I always had to weigh the risk with the reward. That day was no exception.

LUKE WASN'T FOND OF SWIMMING. Whenever Mike and I would be in our pool, Luke would avoid the edge of the pool like the plague. He didn't want to be in a position where we could get to him and make him get in, even if it was only on the large bench-like step into the shallow area. If he were to get in the pool, it had to be on his terms. He would sometimes follow Bella in when they were playing a rousing game of catch-me-if-you-can, and she would try to get away from him by jumping in the pool. Luke often barked at us from the side of the pool, especially if we were splashing around. He didn't particularly like any water other than the water he drank or if there were a tennis ball involved. We had to be sure Luke was in the house when our automatic sprinklers would go on in our backyard because Luke would attack them with a vengeance. He would run from one sprinkler to another and try to tear them out of the ground. Since there were sprinklers all through the grass in the yard, I'm sure he thought he was trying to stop an all-out assault against him. His defensive maneuvers often proved quite costly. We had to keep a supply of sprinkler parts on hand for just such occasions. Using a water hose while Luke was in the vicinity was also a challenge. He especially disliked it if we purposefully splashed him from the pool. He would grab the shoes that we had taken off prior to getting in the water and run off with them. We learned to put them away in a place where Luke couldn't get to them. We found out one day just how much he despised being splashed and how far he would go to exact revenge on anyone who dared to test his limits.

Mike and I were celebrating a special occasion at our home on a beautiful sunny weekend day. The occasion was worth toasting to with a great bottle of champagne. We had a special bottle saved for that very purpose. Rather than going out to celebrate, we stayed home and barbecued a couple of tender juicy steaks and enjoyed them as a late lunch on our back patio. Luke and Bella were at their ever-present spot under the table waiting for any tasty morsels that might escape from our plates. The weather was perfect for swimming, so we put on our swimsuits, got a couple of champagne glasses, poured a glass each and got in the pool. The water was refreshing, and we were happy and relaxed. We raised our glasses and toasted to our accomplishment. Bella joined us in the pool. She generally stayed out of our way, swimming back and forth from end to end of the pool. We invited Luke to join us, but he rudely declined by barking his dissatisfaction with our request. *"Haven't you learned anything by now? You know I don't like to swim,"* Luke must have been thinking. I playfully splashed Mike with pool water. He splashed me back. We couldn't go so far as an all-out water battle as we still had our champagne glasses in our hands. Luke grew more perturbed and began barking much louder. His barking drew our attention and we began splashing water at him. He ran back and forth from one end of the pool to the other, considering whether he should jump in after us or just voice his displeasure. It was then that we saw the look of dawning realization come over Luke's face. He saw an opportunity to hit us right where it hurt.

The moment we saw the vindictive look in Luke's eyes, we knew we were in trouble. Since Luke was the dog who "got it," we had no doubt he was about to exact revenge. We had put our shoes away before getting in the pool, so we thought we were safe. We severely underestimated his desire for retribution for our transgressions against him. How dare we splash him! Luke's eyes darted to an object sitting next to the shallow end of the pool. We followed his gaze. We both gasped. Mike and I knew at once that we had to act fast. We only had one hand each as we were still holding our champagne glasses. We lopsidedly began swimming frantically towards the shallow end, trying desperately to keep our now half-empty champagne glasses above water. We weren't fast enough. Luke had won many races at the dog shows, and we were no match for his quick and nimble athleticism. We watched helplessly as he grabbed the neck of the nearly full champagne bottle we had left on the pool deck, tilted it sideways and promptly ran off with it. We called futilely to him from the pool, but he was on a mission...a mission to exact revenge upon us for our indiscretions towards him. We painfully watched as the precious liquid ran from the bottle while Luke proudly ran around the yard, bottle in his mouth, having his own celebration. He was practically dancing with delight. Much of being successful in battle is knowing your enemy's weak spot. Luke hit us where it hurt that day.

MIKE AND I GET ALONG VERY WELL. We love sharing adventures during the day and then discussing them while preparing our dinner in the evenings. We think alike on many subjects, but there are some on which we don't share the same opinion. We have no problem letting each other know just what that opinion is, and why it's the best one. I have nicknamed us "The Bickersons" for our ability to bicker back and forth about anything we disagree on. It's normally fun and challenging for us. We usually don't take it seriously, but on one occasion I can recall, we let our bickering get out of hand. I can't for the life of me remember what point we were trying so hard to convince the other of, but I do remember that we got to the boiling point in a verbal argument. It happened in our kitchen while we were making dinner. We were both yelling very loudly at each other, trying to convince the other of our side of the argument. The deafening sound of our voices soon reached a fever pitch. We had reached an impasse in our heated discussion and were on the brink of throwing a verbal dagger that could possibly end up being something we couldn't take back, when out of the blue we heard a resounding and powerful bark come from the area of our feet. It was the loudest and most commanding bark we had ever heard. We both immediately stopped screaming at each other and looked down. Luke was staring up at us with a steely expression. He looked from me to Mike and back again with stern consternation. It was obvious to us that Luke was very disappointed in our behavior. That one solitary bark said it all. *"Knock it off you guys! Look at how you're talking to each other. You're acting like fools. I don't want to hear one more word out of you. Say you're sorry to each other and make up. Now!"* We looked at Luke and then at each other. We both started to laugh uncontrollably. There was no doubt we had just been scolded and schooled by our dog. Luke was right. He "got it." We *had* been acting like fools. That single, solitary bark brought us back to our senses.

Family photo day.

LUKE SLEPT IN BED WITH ME for most of his life. When he was a puppy, he would sleep on my pillow just above my head. When he was what I would consider a toddler, he moved his sleeping spot to the crook of my left arm, between my armpit and elbow. In his adolescence, he once again moved to sleeping on my left side just above my hip. In his young adulthood, he was sleeping in the crooks of my knees. When he was middle aged, he slept at the foot of the bed next to my ankles. As Luke got older, he lost much of his eyesight and hearing. This didn't happen until he was almost sixteen years old. At this point, he moved off of the bed to the loveseat that sat at the foot of the bed. When he could no longer safely jump on or off of the loveseat, he began to sleep on the floor next to my side of the bed. I had to be extremely careful not to step on him if I had to get up in the middle of the night for any reason. He didn't like to be startled and would lash out in fear and snap to protect himself if that happened.

LUKE WAS THE FIRST DOG TO INTRODUCE ME TO FRAPs (Frenetic Random Activity Periods), or Zoomies, as I have heard them called more recently. Mike and I called them "going crazy." For apparently no reason whatsoever, Luke would run around a room or rooms as fast as his legs could carry him. The only time I could reliably predict a FRAP was just after I gave Luke a bath. I would towel him off and then he would take off like a rabbit running away from a hungry coyote. He would run around the house at full speed with his butt tucked under him, sliding on the tile floors as he made a sudden turn in direction or rounded a corner. He'd jump onto the family room couch in a single bound, leap up to the top and launch himself as far as he could onto the floor. From there he would run around the recliners, under the dining room table, around the kitchen island, and then back to the family room where he would repeat the sequence over and over until he tired himself out. We would cheer him on, yelling *"Go Luke go!"* The next day would be an entirely different FRAP route. He never really repeated the same route twice, and he never stopped entertaining us with his FRAPs. Even though he eventually went almost completely blind, he somehow managed to navigate a FRAP with ease. He wasn't as fast as he once was, but he went faster during his going crazy FRAPS than we ever expected of him. He had to show us that he still had it. He was the racing champion at many shows for a reason.

LUKE WAS A HEALTHY DOG throughout his lifetime. Other than going partially blind and deaf in his later senior years, there weren't many occasions which required a visit to the vet other than for an annual checkup and vaccinations. On one of those rare visits, Mike and I took Luke to be seen because he seemed to be having trouble chewing his kibble, and he was becoming more and more disinterested in his food. That was completely out of character for Luke who could gulp down an entire dog food "pie" in the blink of an eye. We suspected that he had a dental issue. I attempted to open Luke's mouth to see what I could see. He was having nothing of it and growled and snapped at me, letting me know his mouth was off-limits and surely painful. I think he actually tried to remove several of my fingers. I couldn't muzzle him in order to get a better look because the problem was in his mouth. I knew he was in pain. We decided it would be best to take him to see our regular vet. He happened to be out of the office that week. The front desk staff assured us that we would be in good hands with another vet in the office. We knew our regular vet was familiar with Luke and his personality. We were escorted into one of the examination rooms and waited nervously to meet the unfortunate vet who would soon be examining the inside of an angry lion's mouth. Well, that's what it seemed like to us. The vet came in, introduced himself and asked what the problem was with Luke. We related to him that we thought Luke might have a bad tooth or something else going on his mouth due to his behavior and reduced appetite. The vet concurred and said he would have to take a closer look inside of Luke's mouth to be sure. We warned him extensively about Luke's lightning quick ability to strike and take out a supposed enemy, such as squirrels and gardeners. He just smiled and asked us to put Luke on the exam table. He spoke softly to Luke and patiently told him he wanted to look at his teeth. We were thinking those words might just be the last words he would ever speak. As he reached toward Luke's mouth, Mike and I both anxiously held our breath and watched wide-eyed. I wanted to cover my face with my hands but thought better of it. We stared in utter disbelief as the vet placed his hands over Luke's mouth, pulling up Luke's lips in order to get a better look at his teeth. He ran his fingers over Luke's gums, without one bit of resistance from him, and then an even more unbelievable thing happened. Without having been prompted, Luke opened his mouth widely so the vet could get a good look inside. The vet had his face almost completely inside of the powerful jaws of the lion. I began to wonder if we had enough insurance to cover us if Luke swallowed the vet whole in one gargantuan bite. It would be the nightmare version of the dog food pie-eating contest. It was incredibly difficult to watch, but as it turned out, we were worried about nothing. It was as if Luke were pointing out the offending tooth to the vet. He was saying, *"It's this one right back here. It's been hurting like a son-of-a-gun. Can you help me?"* Mike and I couldn't believe our eyes. We should have though, because Luke once again "got it." He knew he needed help and this new vet was the one to deliver it. The vet confirmed it. Luke did have a very bad tooth that required removal. He never ceased to amaze me.

Say Cheese! Now that's a toothy smile.
Luke celebrated his 15th birthday with a cake made especially for dogs.

MIKE AND I LIVED IN A COMMUNITY surrounded by wine grapes. The grapevines were used as landscaping, and the grapes were sold to wineries and local home winemakers. We decided to try our hand at making our own wine. Our good friend and neighbor, Grant, co-managed the vineyards in our community and had made his own wine. He agreed to help us make ours. We purchased enough Cabernet Franc grapes to make a barrel of wine. One barrel of wine makes approximately twenty-five cases of bottled wine. We split the final amount with Grant for his gracious and generous help in providing the knowledge and equipment needed to make a successful vintage. That meant Mike and I would have 150 bottles to fill and label.

We made a delectable wine. It took the top prize in our local home winemakers' competition. My ultimate goal in making this wine was to create my own wine label with Luke featured prominently on it. The label I designed had Luke's head set atop a pair of crossbones. I wanted it to look like a skull and crossbones which often symbolize the warning to "stay away." I named the wine "Bad to the Bone" because Luke reminded me of the subject of George Thorogood's song of the same name. If Luke had been human, he would surely have recognized himself in that song.

A good wine (and hopefully all good dogs) can age for a very long time. It has been almost thirteen years since Luke passed, and I still have several bottles of that wine. Every time we open one, we raise our glasses and toast to the most incredible fur kid who gave us many years of happy times and adventures that we will never forget.

WHEN LUKE WAS ALMOST SEVENTEEN years old and almost completely blind, he surprised me one day by bringing me a tennis ball that had been in our backyard. I don't know how or where he found it, but he was so proud of himself for finding it. He set it at my feet and looked up eagerly towards my face. Mike was usually the one to play fetch with him. They hadn't played fetch for well over a year. I knew this was a special moment. I picked up the ball and a look of excitement and extreme joy came over Luke's face. He barked elatedly in his old man's voice, asking why it was taking so long for me to throw the ball. I did exactly as I was told and threw the ball, but not as far as I would normally throw it. I didn't want it to be too difficult for him to find. As soon as the ball left my hand, Luke ran after it like he had when he was just a tiny puppy. He sniffed around for the ball and found it faster than I could ever have imagined. He happily trotted back to me and again dropped it at my feet, eagerly awaiting the next throw. He was happier than I had seen him for a very long time. His dexterity had been declining for some time as he aged, and he had been slowly losing control of his hind legs. Luke had been extremely athletic in his prime years, but all of the jumping and running had gradually caught up with him. I know he wouldn't have regretted one moment of his adventures though. I also believe he suffered from some form of canine dementia once he reached the age of sixteen. As I mentioned, he didn't play fetch for over a year. He would often become disoriented or confused. He would stand for long periods of time simply facing a wall and teetering on his hind legs. He had begun urinating in the house. I knew he wasn't comfortable doing that, but he had a difficult time navigating the dog door to go outside. He wasn't incontinent, but I knew that would probably come next. I was utterly amazed to see that he seemed to have magically regressed back to his youth during our game of fetch that wonderful day. He was running like a deer happily prancing through the woods. That day I saw a youthful dog with 20/20 vision and ears that could hear a mouse eating a breadcrumb from a mile away. For a short period of time, Luke was young again. We played for almost an hour. Mike wasn't home and unfortunately missed the opportunity to play fetch that one last time with Luke. It was magical. It was a gift. I was so honored that Luke gave that to me. It's one of my most treasured memories.

LUKE DIED AT SEVENTEEN YEARS OF AGE, not long after our special play day. He passed away peacefully at home. We had him cremated and had a special urn made to hold his precious ashes. It sits on a shelf in our bedroom (on my side of the bed of course) next to a photo of Luke looking up wide-eyed at me from inside of the groundhog hole when we went hunting together so many years ago. His eyes in the photo are shining with sheer joy and are imploring me to join him in the earthen den below. It's the perfect picture to signify our forever bond.

It is often said that people come into one another's lives for a reason, a season or a lifetime. Luke came into mine for a lifetime. His lifetime. Seventeen years is a long time for a dog to live, but the swiftly moving nature of a dog's life is never long enough for those left behind to grieve for them. The only bad thing about dogs is that they don't live as long as we do. I would often tell Mike that it wouldn't bother me if I left this world before Luke did. If for any reason that happened, Mike had very specific instructions. He knew that he was to bring Luke to the cemetery and let him pee on my headstone. I would be his forever, and he mine.

Luke's fifth birthday. He wasn't fed people food, but we always made an exception on his special day.

Easter Bunny tryout reject.

Santa Luke

Good dogs get Christmas presents from Santa.
(Pictured from left - Luke, Rookie, Jade and Lacey)

Christmas at my mom's house.
Luckily Luke didn't chew up any of her stuffed animals!

Now that's an armful of cuteness!

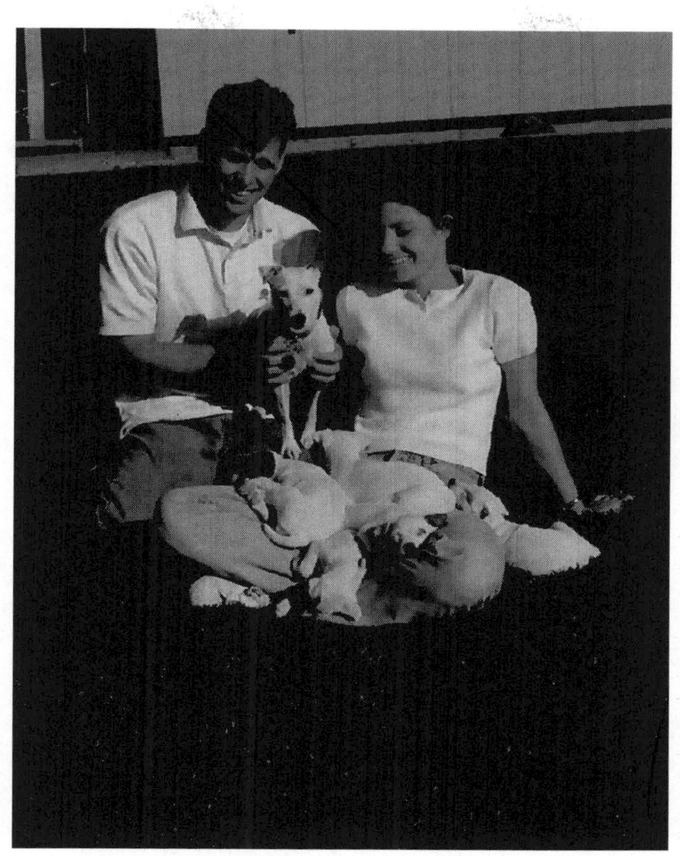

Puppy buyers finding it very hard to choose.

Lacey and Rookie keeping cool on a hot summer day in California.

Chillin'

Sweet Jade. The love of Luke's life.

Oh, how Luke loved this little girl.

Ready to race!

Luke never cared about ribbons,
but he certainly won many throughout the years.

Waiting for our turn in the agility ring.

Luke on his 17th birthday. Still as handsome as ever!

For more information on Jack Russell Terriers

The Jack Russell Terrier Club of America
Website: www.therealjackrussell.com
P.O. Box 4527
Lutherville, MD 21094-4527
Ph: (410) 561-3655
Email: JRTCA@therealjackrussell.com

Special Thanks to...

Deborah Arnold, a successful author of many wonderful books, for her tireless work in editing this book, and providing much needed assistance and encouragement along the way.

Cover Art by Caitlyn Nevitt. She truly captured Luke's spirit and attitude in her painting.

Made in USA - Crawfordsville, IN
63441_9798218025892
03.06.2023 1843